RED INK II

RED INK II

A Guide to Understanding the Continuing Deficit Dilemma

ALFRED J. WATKINS

Introduction by William A. Galston

Hamilton Press

Lanham • New York • London

Roosevelt Center for
American Policy Studies

Library of Congress Cataloging-in-Publication Data

Watkins, Alfred J.
Red ink II : a guide to understanding the continuing deficit
dilemma / Alfred J. Watkins ; introduction by William A. Galston.
p. cm.
1. Budget deficits—United States. 2. Debts, Public—United
States. I. Title. II. Title: Red ink 2. III. Title: Red ink two.
HJ2052.W38   1988
339.5'23'0973—dc 19   87–36000 CIP
ISBN 0–8191–6838–6 (alk. paper)
ISBN 0–8191–6839–4 (pbk. : alk. paper)

All Hamilton Press books are produced on acid-free
paper which exceeds the minimum standards set by the National
Historical Publications and Records Commission.

Hamilton Press

**Roosevelt Center for
American Policy Studies**

Contents

Board of Directors

The goal of the Roosevelt Center is to increase public understanding of critical national policy issues and encourage citizen participation in our country's decision-making process. The Center believes that a questioning, skeptical, and active public is necessary to the proper functioning of our government and our way of life.

While many institutions help inform citizens on policy matters, both the Center's particular mission and the methods it uses to achieve its ends are distinctive. Many citizens want to understand and to be involved in those policy decisions that affect their lives but are discouraged by the lack of reliable information or the profusion of conflicting opinions. The Center's experience shows that if ordinary citizens are given clearly stated information and policy options, free of partisan rhetoric and presented in an interesting and challenging format, many will respond by taking a livelier interest in public affairs.

Through a process the Center calls "public engagement," citizens from across the geographic and political landscape examine key policy issues using teaching tools specially created by the Center. Through Center programs, tens of thousands of citizens across the country—including teachers, students, politicians, and civic leaders—examine selected issues and political processes at close range. Community events include Center-sponsored town meetings, debates, role-playing exercises, and study courses. In keeping with the Center's basic principles, the learning materials it produces for its public engagement activities are rigorously nonprescriptive: they make no attempt to push people toward any preconceived solution.

INTRODUCTION

The Roosevelt Center for American Policy Studies, a non-partisan public policy institution, is pleased to present this updated and expanded edition of its citizen's guide to the federal budget deficit. The publication of this volume could not be more timely. In recent months the political deadlock at the heart of the deficit has been a matter of sharply rising concern, not just for elected officials, but for the American people themselves, who share in the responsibility for this dangerous situation.

During the 1980s, the federal budget deficit soared to levels that would have been unimaginable in previous decades. In the past five years, annual deficits have averaged $195 billion. Not surprisingly, both the national debt and annual interest payments on that debt have soared—in dollars and as a percentage of our gross national product.

Throughout this period of dramatically rising deficits, many experts have warned that the long-term consequences for the U.S. economy could be severe: excessive interest rates, inadequate savings and investment, diminished international competitiveness, a lower standard of living for our children and a loss of control over our very destiny as a nation. But until recently, these warnings fell on deaf ears. After all, the economy had been growing steadily for more than five years, inflation seemed to have been tamed, jobs were being created by the millions, and nominal interest rates, though still high, had been cut by more than half from their peak in the early 1980s.

The 508-point stock market crash of October 19, 1987 changed the outlook of the public and its elected representatives. People began to focus on the growing foreign indebtedness of the United States and on the declining international confidence in the future of the U.S. economy. Opinion polls revealed that the budget deficit had become "Public Enemy Number One." Meanwhile, Congress and the Administration began negotiations designed to achieve meaningful, multi-year reductions in the deficit.

Events soon revealed, however, that the psychological changes set in motion by the stock market were not enough to break the longstanding political deadlock over the deficit. After nearly a month of talks, Congress and the Administration were able to reach agreement on only a modest package of deficit-reduction measures. The public, meanwhile, seemed to be divided against itself. Nearly everyone agreed that the budget deficit was intolerable and had to be slashed. At the same time, most people appeared to reject most of the options for achieving that goal. To judge from the traditional opinion polls, public sentiment could be summed up as follows: "Cut the deficit, but don't raise taxes, don't touch Social Security, shore up the safety net for needy Americans, and expand government-funded health services for the elderly and the victims of catastrophic illness." Under these circumstances, public officials who pushed for major deficit reductions seemed to be risking their political careers. Few did.

In a representative government, elected officials are unlikely to deviate very far from the wishes of their constituents—at least as they understand those wishes. If the deficit deadlock is to be broken, therefore, elected officials will have to start receiving different signals from the citizens who put—and keep—them in office. This depends, in turn, on a higher level of public understanding concerning the dimensions of the deficit problem and the principal options for solving it, and on more effective communication between voters and their representatives. It is the purpose of this book to address the first

need—that is, to provide the basis for improved public understanding by discussing the federal budget deficit in clear,
nontechnical, and nonpartisan terms.

Chapter One provides basic information about the dimensions of the deficit and its evolution over the past generation.
This chapter then examines the principal effects of the deficit
and concludes with an inventory of basic strategies for dealing
with it, ranging from inflation, debt repudiation, and economic
growth to varying ideas about appropriate yearly deficit targets.

Chapter Two discusses the complex process by which our
government formulates its annual budget, including the recently enacted revisions of the Gramm-Rudman-Hollings deficit-reduction act. This chapter also presents the different ways
in which the budget may be subdivided and explains many
puzzling facts—for example, how spending can go up even
when the budget has been "cut," and conversely, why services may have to be slashed even though the budget has been
"increased."

Chapter Three examines where the federal government gets
its money, who pays the taxes currently in effect, and the
implication of the 1986 tax reform legislation. It then sketches
some important options for cutting the budget deficit by raising
revenues, including higher income taxes, new consumption
taxes, and stricter enforcement of the tax code.

Chapter Four examines how the federal government spends
its money and how expenditure patterns have changed over
time. It then discusses some important options for cutting the
budget deficit by reducing spending, including Social Security,
government-supported health care, defense, foreign aid,
"safety net" programs for the disadvantaged, federal retirement, veterans' benefits, and agricultural subsidies.

Chapter Five presents a brief history of federal budget
processes and offers a number of proposals for altering them,
including the line item veto, balanced budget amendment, and
longer-term budgeting procedures. It concludes with the argument that no procedural reforms, however well designed, can

hope to match the positive impact of an aroused and informed citizenry.

Readers of this book will not learn "the" solution for the federal budget deficit. (Indeed, there is no single solution, but only a range of conflicting conceptions that must somehow be harmonized through political processes of debate and deliberation.) Rather, readers will learn what they need to know to clarify their own judgment and make up their own minds.

Improved individual understanding of the federal budget deficit is the essential first step. But it is only the beginning. Citizens must also find ways of deliberating jointly, of forging consensus, and of transmitting their judgments to their elected representatives and other key policymakers. Through its DEBTBUSTERS exercise and through nationwide organizing efforts linked to both Congressional budget debates and the 1988 presidential campaign, the Roosevelt Center has tried to provide arenas for meaningful citizen discussions and to build bridges between informed citizens and their leaders. The results have consistently shown that, when confronted with the whole of the deficit dilemma, citizens are prepared to agree upon balanced packages of deficit reduction measures which, taken one by one, many of them would regard as unacceptable. The Center intends to continue these efforts until citizens across this country have had the opportunity they deserve to make their voices heard—effectively—in our nation's Capitol.

The stakes are very high. If citizens take the trouble to inform themselves and then transmit their considered judgments—as opposed to the instant opinions registered by opinion polls—to their elected representatives, there is hope that progress can be made. If citizens do not do this, the U.S. deficit deadlock of the 1980s is all too likely to persist indefinitely, with grave consequences both for our country and for the world.

William A. Galston
Director, Economic and Social Programs
Roosevelt Center for American
Policy Studies
December, 1987

CHAPTER 1

Debts and Deficits

THE NATURE AND SIZE OF THE FEDERAL DEFICIT AND DEBT

Practically every American understands what it means to be in debt. Most Americans go into debt when they purchase homes and cars. Many also pay for such everyday consumption items as vacations and clothing with credit cards. They recognize that when they borrow, they will be required to pay interest. They also know that the principal must eventually be repaid as well.

Despite these repayment obligations, Americans borrowed considerable sums in recent years. In 1986, U.S. households borrowed more than $290 billion, raising their total debt by year end to more than $2,650 billion. They had over $1,600 billion in outstanding mortgage debt on residential properties, which amounts to slightly less than $10,000 for every man and woman in the U.S. over the age of 16. Outstanding consumer credit, such as auto loans and charge card balances, amounted to nearly $730 billion or about $4,500 for each person over the age of 16. Consequently, the average adult is obliged to spend well over $1,000 every year merely to pay interest on this debt.

People incur debt because their needs for consumption or investment, at least as they define them, exceed their current resources. They go into debt believing that when the debts come due, they will have more than enough income to pay what is owed and still have enough left over to maintain their

1

living standards. Corporations operate the same way when
they borrow to enlarge their inventories and purchase new
machinery and equipment. They assume that their investments
will generate more than enough additional revenue to retire the
debt and still leave the firm with a profit.

Government officials resort to borrowing for many of the
same reasons. When their immediate needs appear to exceed
their available resources, borrowing can be an attractive way
to plug the gap.

Americans have long feared that their democratically-
elected public officials would try to increase their popularity
at the expense of sound fiscal management. Politicians, it was
believed, would try to curry favor with the voters by enacting
new spending programs. But those same officials would refuse
to enact the politically unpopular tax increases needed to
finance those spending programs. As a result, there would be
a built-in tendency for spending to rise faster than revenues,
leading to a constant stream of deficits. In other words, because democratic governments would try to finance a portion
of their spending programs by borrowing rather than taxing,
the bill for their profligacy would be passed on to future
generations.

In order to restrain politicians, the constitutions of practically every American state contain provisions prohibiting operating deficits. Generally, state officials can borrow only to
finance long-term capital outlays. In some states, even this
requires direct voter approval. Many state laws also prohibit
cities and counties from running unbalanced budgets as well.

Federal Borrowing

The federal government is not bound by the same anti-deficit
rules and regulations. Every year, Congress' decisions about
the shape of the tax code helps to determine how much
revenue the federal government will receive. Congress also
passes appropriations bills and authorizes entitlements which
determine how much money the federal government will spend
each year. (See the following chapter for a more detailed

discussion of the budget process.) However, when the federal government makes its budget, income does not have to equal outgo. Consequently, at least in recent years, deficits are not only possible but probable.

Public opinion surveys consistently show that Americans want the federal government to balance its budget. President Reagan says he supports a balanced budget. So did Walter Mondale, his opponent in the 1984 election. Nor does it seem likely that any of the candidates running for President in 1988 will oppose balancing the federal budget and support continued, large deficits. Many state legislatures feel so strongly about the need for a balanced budget that more than 30 have passed resolutions calling on Congress to add a balanced budget amendment to the Constitution.

Throughout most of American history, the federal government incurred deficits primarily to fight wars, generating a balanced budget or surplus the rest of the time. From the founding of our nation until 1850, there was, on average, a surplus. In the following 50 years, which included the Civil War, the total deficit was under a billion dollars. The government went about $22 billion in debt to finance World War I but wiped much of that out with surpluses in the 1920s.

During the Great Depression of the 1930s, annual deficits rose again, but never exceeded $4.4 billion. Then came World War II, when the deficit peaked at $54 billion. At the end of that war, our national debt was $260 billion. In the 1960s, the annual deficit was held to under $7 billion every year except at the height of the Vietnam War, and there were surpluses in two years.

In the 1970s, deficits began to grow, exceeding $70 billion under both Presidents Ford and Carter. In 1981, President Reagan proposed major tax cuts for individuals and corporations, to which the Congress made significant additions. It had been hoped that these tax cuts would so stimulate the economy that balanced budgets would be possible. Instead, the nation went into one of its worst recessions, which cut federal revenues while increasing spending. The result was large and growing deficits, measured both in terms of dollars and as a percentage of GNP (Table 1.1).

Future Deficits

Large deficits are now built into the federal budget. The Congressional Budget Office (CBO) predicts that by 1991, if Congress neither raises taxes nor alters current domestic

TABLE 1.1
FEDERAL BUDGET DEFICITS

	Budget Surplus or Deficit (−) ($ Billions)	Surplus or Deficit as % of GNP		Budget Surplus or Deficit (−) ($ Billions)	Surplus or Deficit as % of GNP
1946	−15.9	−7.5	1971	−23.0	−2.2
1947	4.0	1.8	1972	−23.4	−2.0
1948	11.8	4.8	1973	−14.9	−1.2
1949	.6	.2	1974	−6.1	−.4
1950	−3.1	−1.2	1975	−53.2	−3.5
1951	6.1	1.9	1976	−73.7	−4.3
1952	−1.5	−.4	1977	−53.6	−2.8
1953	−6.4	−1.8	1978	−59.2	−2.7
1954	−1.1	−.3	1979	−40.2	−1.6
1955	−3.0	−.8	1980	−73.8	−2.8
1956	3.9	.9	1981	−78.9	−2.6
1957	3.4	.8	1982	−127.9	−4.1
1958	−2.7	−.6	1983	−208.9	−6.3
1959	−12.8	−2.7	1984	−185.3	−5.0
1960	.3	.1	1985	−212.3	−5.4
1961	−3.3	−.6	1986	−220.7	−5.3
1962	−7.1	−1.3	1987	−148.0	−3.4
1963	−4.7	−.8	1988 (proj.)	−183.0	−3.9
1964	−5.9	−.9	1989 (proj.)	−192.0	−3.8
1965	−1.4	−.2	1990 (proj.)	−176.0	−3.3
1966	−3.7	−.5	1991 (proj.)	−165.0	−2.9
1967	−8.6	−1.1			
1968	−25.1	−3.0			
1969	3.2	.3			
1970	−2.8	−.3			

spending patterns, and if the President's defense buildup is fully funded, revenues will be $1,115 billion but spending will be $1,280 billion, leaving a deficit of $165 billion.

Experts differ on the precise magnitude of future deficits, but they all agree that if current policies are not changed, the resulting deficits will continue to be large. In August 1987, the Congressional Budget Office estimated that continuing current services and taxes would produce a cumulative deficit of $716 billion during the four fiscal years beginning in October 1987. (These projected deficits are listed in Table 1.1.) These estimates assume that there will be no recession between now and 1991 or that if one does occur, its effects will be offset by a rapid and strong recovery. If the recession is steeper, or the recovery weaker, future deficits will be even larger.

The "Off-the-Books" Deficit

Most estimates of how much the federal government runs in the red don't include deficits carried in "off-budget" accounts. By law, the spending isn't included in the budget totals and thus doesn't affect the reported deficit. These items typically total from $10 billion to $20 billion a year.

A more serious omission is hidden liabilities for Social Security and other retirement programs. When a company has a pension plan, it is required to put aside money each year for its current workers to build up a fund for their retirement. This ensures that even if a company goes bankrupt, there is enough money set aside so that its retired workers will get their pensions. The federal government doesn't have a similar requirement for Social Security. Instead, the payroll taxes paid by workers and their employers are used to pay benefits to those already retired. Today's workers will have to get their pensions when they retire from those who are still working. If the federal government had to follow the practices it requires of private companies, the federal debt for pensions would be listed in the trillions.

Sources of the Deficit

The very high budget deficits experienced during the 1980s can be explained quite simply: as Table 1.2 indicates, while spending continued to rise in a number of areas, taxes stabilized as a fraction of gross national product (GNP).

A further breakdown of these averages reveals some interesting trends. In the nondefense portion of the budget, spending for entitlement programs (primarily Social Security and Medicare) has risen in line with GNP over the past five years, consuming 10.8% in 1981 and 11.0% in 1986. During this same period, spending for discretionary programs (for example, housing, transportation, aid to the poor, and environmental protection) dropped from 5.6% of GNP to 4.1%. Meanwhile, interest on the national debt surged from 2.3% of GNP to 3.3%.

TABLE 1.2

FEDERAL FINANCES, SPENDING, AND RECEIPTS AS A PERCENTAGE OF GNP

	Defense	Non-Defense	Total	Receipts
1950s Average	10.7	7.5	18.2	17.8
1960s Average	9.1	10.3	19.4	18.6
1970–1974 Average	7.0	13.0	20.0	18.8
1975–1979 Average	5.2	16.8	22.0	19.0
1985	6.5	17.8	24.3	19.1
1986	6.6	17.2	23.8	18.5

The Size of the Debt

The total national debt on October 1, 1987, was just under $2.3 trillion. But the federal government itself holds a significant proportion of this debt in its trust funds for Social Security and other purposes, so most people focus on "debt held by the public." That debt estimate for October 1987 was $1.9 trillion. If current tax and spending policies are continued without change, the debt held by the public will grow to $2.6 trillion by October 1991, according to CBO.

TABLE 1.3
FEDERAL DEBT HELD BY THE PUBLIC
($ Billions)

	Debt Held by Public	Ratio of Debt to GNP		Debt Held by Public	Ratio of Debt to GNP
1946	241.9	1.14	1971	304.3	.29
1947	224.3	1.00	1972	323.8	.28
1948	216.3	.87	1973	343.0	.27
1949	214.3	.81	1974	346.1	.24
1950	219.0	.82	1975	396.9	.26
1951	214.3	.68	1976	480.3	.28
1952	214.8	.63	1977	551.8	.29
1953	218.4	.60	1978	610.9	.28
1954	224.5	.61	1979	644.6	.26
1955	226.6	.59	1980	715.1	.27
1956	222.2	.53	1981	794.4	.27
1957	219.4	.50	1982	929.4	.30
1958	226.4	.50	1983	1141.8	.34
1959	235.0	.49	1984	1312.6	.36
1960	237.2	.47	1985	1509.9	.38
1961	238.6	.46	1986	1746.1	.42
1962	248.4	.45	1987	1901.0	.43
1963	254.5	.43	1988 (proj.)	2077.0	.44
1964	257.6	.41	1989 (proj.)	2266.0	.45
1965	261.6	.39	1990 (proj.)	2440.0	.45
1966	264.7	.36	1991 (proj.)	2601.0	.45
1967	267.5	.34			
1968	290.6	.34			
1969	279.5	.30			
1970	284.9	.29			

One way of understanding such large numbers is to allocate the debt to each worker in the United States. The October 1987 debt is about $15,000 per worker. If current policies continue, it will rise to approximately $20,000 per worker by October of 1991.

The debt is like a good investment in reverse. A good investment compounds: it pays interest, which adds to the amount invested, which increases the interest, which further increases the amount invested, which increases the interest, and so on. The debt, on the other hand, creates interest costs which add to the principal owed, which increases the interest costs, which increases the principal owed, and so on. In 1986, the interest bill on the national debt was $136 billion, or about $1,100 per worker. This bill will rise as each annual deficit increases the size of the debt held by the public. Under current policies and projected interest rates, annual interest payments are expected to be $179 billion by 1991, or about $1,400 per worker.

THE EFFECTS OF DEFICITS AND DEBT

The widespread impression that unbalanced federal budgets have become a way of life has triggered considerable interest in understanding the economic consequences of perpetual deficits and rising federal debt. While economists and others who have studied the subject do not always agree on the details, all of them believe that large, persistent government deficits have significant economic impacts.

Deficits and the Business Cycle

One of the reasons it is difficult to have a balanced budget every year is that the business cycle—the periodic cycling of recession and growth—has a major impact on the government's expenditures and revenues. During recessions, the federal budget experiences both a loss of revenues and increased spending. Slower growth in personal income means less revenue from the individual income tax; more unemployment means less Social Security payroll tax revenues; and lower corporate profits mean lower corporate tax receipts. On the spending side, high unemployment increases unemployment compensation costs as well as the cost of welfare programs. Thus, when the pace of economic growth slows, revenues decline and spending rises. When economic growth accelerates, the process is reversed. Spending declines while revenues rise.

Because deficits rise during recessions and fall during recoveries, some economists believe that the federal budget actually works like an economic balance wheel or "automatic stabilizer," helping to regulate the pace of economic activity and dampening the swings of the business cycle. During recessions, having the government put more money into the economy (by spending) than it takes out (by taxing) stimulates aggregate demand. This in turn reduces the severity of the recession and hastens the onset of a recovery. During recoveries, deficits decline, leaving more resources available for private consumption and investment.

According to this perspective, deficits *per se* are not detrimental and at times can actually be economically beneficial. But persistent deficits in prosperous times are not so benign. When the economy is operating at close to full capacity, the extra spending represented by the deficit leads to rising prices, not higher output and productivity. In addition, government borrowing at this stage of the recovery "crowds out" private sector borrowing, leaving fewer resources with which to finance new production facilities.

As the following table indicates, the deficit has neither increased nor decreased significantly between 1983 and 1986. Nevertheless, when the effects of the business cycle are removed, we can see that the deficit has, in fact, undergone an enormous change—one which is much more significant than is apparent merely from looking at the actual deficit itself.

In Table 1.4, generated with U.S. Department of Commerce data, the deficit is divided into two components. The first component shows the effects of the business cycle on the deficit. It indicates that this "cyclical" component of the deficit peaked in 1983, when the economy was emerging from the depths of the steepest recession since the Great Depression.

But as the economy entered the recovery phase, the cyclical component of the deficit began to decline as it typically does when the economy picks up steam. Nevertheless, the overall deficit remained steady, primarily because Congress enacted President Reagan's program of tax cuts and higher defense spending, but balked at cutting domestic programs. The result

TABLE 1.4
BUSINESS CYCLES AND THE BUDGET DEFICIT
($ Billions)

	Actual Budget Deficit	Policy Component of Deficit	Cyclical Component of Deficit
1977	53.6	45.7	7.9
1978	59.2	46.4	12.8
1979	40.2	37.1	3.1
1980	73.8	58.5	15.3
1981	78.9	55.4	23.5
1982	127.9	87.2	40.7
1983	208.9	123.8	85.1
1984	185.3	165.2	20.1
1985	212.3	202.3	10.0
1986	220.7	218.6	2.1

was that by 1986, virtually all of the deficit was due to policy decisions since the cyclical component had been eliminated by four years of recovery.

Living on Credit

The main impact of debt on the finances of our government is much like the impact of debt on the finances of a family: it makes a big difference whether the debt is incurred to finance long-term investment or immediate consumption.

Most family debt is incurred to finance the purchase of items that will provide enjoyment over a number of years. This debt has two important characteristics: (1) the value of the capital asset being financed exceeds the debt and (2) the debt is paid off on a schedule that normally means the asset will have some useful life after the debt is repaid. This kind of debt can also be seen as a way of avoiding other costs by paying interest. For example, incurring the cost of interest on a mortgage saves the cost of paying rent.

If the government followed this policy, it would borrow only to finance its purchases of such long-lived investment items as federal dams, public buildings, and such weapons as aircraft carriers, SDI, tanks, etc. And in fact, until recently, borrowing to finance these sorts of civilian and military investments was responsible for a significant fraction of annual government deficits.

Table 1.5 shows how much money the government spent each year on capital equipment. It also shows what the deficit would have been if these capital items were excluded from our calculation of "the deficit." A negative number indicates that the budget, excluding capital expenditures, was actually in surplus.

Analyzing the deficit from this perspective reveals that the budget was much closer to balance than many people realize, at least between 1967 and 1981. Until 1974, the government was actually running an operating surplus. From 1974 to 1981, the operating deficit was much less than the total deficit. However, the operating deficit doubled between 1981 and 1982. It doubled again between 1982 and 1983, and generally has stayed above the $120 billion level ever since. Nevertheless, even at these lofty levels, it is clear that once the capital expenditures are removed from the calculation of the deficit, the remaining deficit is much smaller than the overall deficit.

TABLE 1.5
GOVERNMENT INVESTMENT AND BUDGET DEFICITS
($ Billions)

	Capital Expenditures	Remaining Deficit		Capital Expenditures	Remaining Deficit
1967	24.4	− 15.80	1977	27.3	26.30
1968	28.3	− 3.20	1978	30.0	29.20
1969	28.8	− 32.00	1979	36.5	3.70
1970	26.1	− 23.30	1980	40.5	33.30
1971	23.7	− .70	1981	47.9	31.00
1972	22.7	.70	1982	56.4	71.50
1973	21.3	− 6.40	1983	67.2	141.70
1974	21.3	− 15.20	1984	78.0	107.30
1975	23.5	29.70	1985	89.7	122.60
1976	24.5	49.20	1986	95.9	124.80

However, because so much of the deficit in the past few years is for financing operating expenses, it is also clear that recent federal borrowing is less like a family that borrows to purchase home or a car and more analogous to a family that spends $2,000 a year more than it earns in order to pay for fancy clothes, meals in gourmet restaurants, and a luxury vacation.

Such a family can increase its living standard temporarily, particularly if it can get new loans to pay off old ones. But, in the second year (assuming a 10% interest rate) it would have to borrow $2,200—$2,000 for another year of living beyond its income and $200 to pay interest on the first year's borrowing. Continuing on this course, the family would have to borrow more and more just to maintain its standard of living. Borrowing $2,000 a year to maintain a lifestyle, plus enough more each year to cover the interest, would result in interest costs of about $2,000 in the fifth year and $6,000 in the tenth year.

The math of compounding interest bills is much the same for the U.S. government. In just five years (1981–1986), interest on the national debt has grown from $68.7 billion to $136 billion. In addition, as Table 1.6 shows, interest costs of the federal debt are consuming an increasing share of our national output (GNP). Interest represented 1.4% of GNP in FY 1973. By 1986, that figure had more than doubled, rising to 3.3%.

The CBO predicts that interest expenses will rise to $179 billion, or 3.1% of GNP by 1991, assuming Congress makes no changes in either tax or spending policies. These CBO projections assume that real economic growth will continue at a favorable pace and that interest rates will remain moderate. If they do not, CBO's pessimistic forecast suggests that, by 1991, annual interest payments will rise to well above $200 billion, or approximately 4% of GNP. This scenario may be unduly pessimistic, but the results have one major similarity no matter which of the two sets of assumptions is used: interest burdens rise over time for a government running constant operating deficits, just like they do for a family.

Families could not indefinitely maintain their lifestyle this way because before long, creditors would cease lending to

TABLE 1.6
INTEREST ON THE FEDERAL DEBT
($ Billions and Percentage of GNP)

	Interest Payments on National Debt	Interest Payments as Percent of GNP
1967	10.3	1.30
1968	11.1	1.31
1969	12.7	1.37
1970	14.4	1.45
1971	14.8	1.40
1972	15.5	1.34
1973	17.3	1.35
1974	21.4	1.51
1975	23.2	1.52
1976	26.7	1.57
1977	29.9	1.55
1978	35.4	1.63
1979	42.6	1.74
1980	52.5	1.97
1981	68.7	2.30
1982	85.0	2.71
1983	89.8	2.70
1984	111.1	3.01
1985	129.4	3.29
1986	136.0	3.27
1987	137.0	3.11
1988	150.0	3.19
1989	161.0	3.20
1990	170.0	3.14
1991	179.0	3.09

them. The question is whether there is any difference when governments live beyond their means. One difference is that our government has, everyone assumes, an excellent credit rating, so it has not yet had to face the prospect of being turned away by lenders as a bad risk. Neither a bank nor a friend would be likely to loan much money to a private individual who wanted to live beyond his means indefinitely. But the federal government has the legal ability to raise funds as needed.

Taxes are not automatic, however. Lenders must believe that decisionmakers in the White House and Congress have not only the power to tax and reduce non-interest spending, but also the willingness to use those powers in order to make interest payments. If their willingness to do this comes into question, the financial markets would demand much higher interest rates for loans to the federal government.

Another difference is that as the most credit worthy borrower, the government can usually get a lower interest rate than any private borrower. The result is that the government's debt can still skyrocket—but a little less rapidly than a family's.

Foreign Ownership of American Debt

Another major difference, according to some economists, is that we owe our debt to ourselves. Less than 20% of the outstanding federal debt is directly financed by loans from foreigners; the rest is owed to Americans. But the large deficits of the past several years are rapidly changing this relationship. In 1984, American finances became like those of a less developed country—as a result of the government's continuing budget deficits plus the heavy borrowing by households and businesses, the U.S. borrowed more from foreigners than it invested abroad (Table 1.7). In 1986, the U.S. became the world's largest debtor nation, owing $250 billion more to foreigners than they owe to us.

When Americans borrow from abroad, it is just like a family borrowing from a bank. The interest payments and any repayments of principal reduce the money available to maintain current standards of living. The larger the debt, the higher the share of income that must be used to pay the interest. Many economists now believe that by 1991 or shortly thereafter, the U.S. could owe foreigners close to one trillion dollars and would be obliged to pay them approximately $70 billion each year just in interest. To finance those interest payments, Amer-

TABLE 1.7

NET ASSET POSITION OF THE U.S.
($ Billions)

	Net Creditor or Debtor (-) Position of U.S.		Net Creditor or Debtor (-) Position of U.S.		Net Creditor or Debtor (-) Position of U.S.
1970	58.4	1976	83.5	1982	136.2
1971	45.5	1977	72.7	1983	88.4
1972	37.0	1978	76.1	1984	4.3
1973	47.9	1979	94.4	1985	− 107.4
1974	58.7	1980	106.0	1986	− 263.6
1975	74.2	1981	140.7	1987	− 400.0

icans will have to produce nearly $70 billion more than they consume, leading to a reduction in the average family's annual income of approximately $1,000.

American Ownership of Federal Debt—Who Benefits and Who Pays

When the federal debt is financed domestically, this export of interest abroad does not take place. Instead of siphoning money out of our economy, interest payments shift resources within the economy. But the people earning the interest are by and large different from the ones who are paying taxes to pay the interest.

Some federal debt is held by state and local governments investing temporarily idle funds; some by individuals; but most is held by institutions—banks, savings and loans, company pension plans, insurance companies, and industrial companies with money to invest. So the interest on debt goes primarily to these types of institutions.

To some extent, we all benefit from this interest if we have life insurance policies, private pension plans, or interest- bearing deposits in banks. But how much we benefit depends on how large our stakes are. Those who benefit most are the ones who own stock in banks and other financial institutions, large depositors, and those with large pensions and life insurance policies.

Personal net worth provides a good index of relative benefits. That is, on average, one would expect someone with net worth of half a million to receive at least 100 times as much in federal interest payments as someone with a net worth of $5,000. And since many Americans have negligible (or even negative) net worth, they do not receive any benefit at all from the government's interest payments.

Rather than saying that we owe the federal debt to ourselves, it is more accurate to say that the debt is, on balance, owed by taxpayers to bondholders—or by those who pay federal taxes (now and in the future) to those who already have wealth.

The table below shows shares of payments of federal income tax in 1985 in relation to adjusted gross income. Clearly, the bulk of tax revenues are raised from middle-income taxpayers.

The table does not include Social Security payroll taxes because there is a limit on the amount of income subject to tax; no progressivity in its rate; and no deductions, exemptions, or credits allowed. As a result, poorer persons pay a larger proportion of their incomes in Social Security taxes than those making over $40,000 a year. If these tax payments were added to the table, the share of total taxes paid by middle and low income families would be even higher than the shares shown above.

TABLE 1.8
INCOME TAX REVENUES BY INCOME GROUP

Adjusted Gross Income	Percentage of Total Income Tax Paid by this Group
0-11,000	2.2
11-22,000	11.1
22-35,000	18.3
35-50,000	20.3
50-100,000	23.6
100-200,000	9.1
200-1,000,000	9.7
Over 1,000,000	5.3

You can figure where you stand personally by thinking about your tax return last year. To begin with, you had direct gains and losses from interest payments. Your income from capital (investment) is what you received in interest and dividends. Your payment for capital (debt) is what you paid in interest.

You also paid and received interest indirectly. Assuming earmarked taxes like Social Security are not used to finance the government's interest payments, about 40% of your federal income tax payments were used to pay interest on the federal debt. If you rent, much of your payment covers your owner's interest costs. But you had interest gains that don't appear on your tax form from appreciation in life insurance policies with cash value, from individual retirement accounts (IRAs) and Keogh plans, and from private pension reserves.

Intergenerational Effects

Higher interest on growing federal debt has important implications for the living standards of younger and older persons. Young workers just starting out in life tend to be borrowers. Many borrow to finance their education, borrow again for a car, go deeply into debt to buy a house if they can, then face the massive costs of raising children. Most are hard pressed financially until their children leave home. By then, their salaries have risen, their mortgages are close to being paid off, and their obligations to their children have decreased. At this point, they have money to lend. Their savings are encouraged by the government through such provisions as the special tax treatment of capital gains and tax free interest on IRAs. (These devices provide no help, of course, to those hard pressed people who still need all their income to pay current living expenses.) Thus, higher interest rates tend to transfer resources from younger to older workers.

When people retire, all of their income is derived from capital in some form—rent for any property they own, dividends on stocks, interest on bonds and money funds, and income from investments in company pension plans. Anything that tends to increase interest rates, such as high and persistent government deficits, will have the effect of enriching this group and transferring money from younger to older persons.

Effects on Federal Programs

So long as the government spends more than it takes in, interest costs will continue to rise, making it harder and harder to avoid future deficits. One consequence is increased pressure on Congress to scale back other programs. In recent years, the programs undergoing the highest percentage cuts have been those benefiting younger and poorer members of society, while programs for the middle class and the elderly have been subjected to smaller cuts.

Effects of Deficits on Interest Rates

When the government finances its deficit by borrowing large sums, it comes into competition with other borrowers. These include businesses trying to expand their factories and finance inventories, and people seeking to finance their home mortgages and car loans.

All these potential borrowers are bidding for the opportunity to make use of savings available for lending. These include people who save some of their money in bank deposits, savings and loan shares, certificates of deposit, and bonds. Businesses also save when they establish pension funds for their employees and when they pay out less for operating costs, new facilities, and dividends than they take in from sales. State and local governments save through their retirement funds and budget surpluses, if any. Insurance companies are also a major source of savings because they collect money now to cover payments that often don't have to be made for many years.

Interest rates are the mechanisms that equalize the amounts borrowed and lent. If the amount of savings is greater than the amount that people wish to borrow, interest rates will decline. This encourages more people to borrow and fewer to save until the two are brought back into equilibrium. On the other hand, if there are more borrowers than lenders, interest rates will tend to rise, discouraging borrowing and encouraging saving.

Assume that the economy is operating with no federal deficit. Some people would be borrowing and some lending. Of course, the amount saved would be the same as the amount borrowed. Now imagine that the federal government decides to run a $200 billion annual deficit, thereby increasing the demand for borrowed funds by approximately one-third.

The federal decision to borrow $200 billion will not automatically encourage additional savings. People will not alter their savings for retirement, down payments, or college educations merely because the government decided it wants to increase the amount of money it borrows. Similarly, corporate cash flow will not be increased, nor will contributions to pension plans.

Of course, with a higher demand for borrowed funds and no additional supply of funds to lend, interest rates will increase, thereby discouraging some of the potential borrowers and encouraging more saving. Nevertheless, it is difficult to get people and companies to save more just because the interest rate is a little higher:

• People do not often change their payroll deductions for savings or take fewer vacations just because interest rates are slightly higher.

• Although government spending may boost profits in certain industries, the government deficit does not make company profits as a whole any higher nor dividends any lower, so company savings, in the short run at least, do not respond to higher interest rates.

• Pension commitments of employers are unchanged and so are the schedules by which they accumulate money in pension plans.

For the most part, therefore, the balancing of borrowing and lending comes about not by increasing the savings rate, but rather by driving off some of the potential borrowers through higher interest rates. This happens quickly for some borrowers. The willingness of a mortgage company to extend a housing loan depends on whether loan officers think a potential borrower can service that mortgage. They make this determination by comparing the borrower's monthly income and monthly mortgage payment. Higher interest rates increase the mortgage payment without necessarily increasing the borrower's income, so some people lose their chance to get a mortgage. Higher rates also discourage investment because they increase the costs of financing new plants and equipment without necessarily increasing their expected profitability. As a result, as interest rates rise, some investment projects that seemed profitable at a lower rate of interest no longer make economic sense.

Effects of High Interest Rates

High interest rates have very different effects on people in different situations, even when the economy as a whole is performing nicely. To make a long story short, they explain why many people are out of work in the lumber industry in Oregon, the textile industry in the Carolinas, and the steel industry in the Midwest.

High interest rates tend to discourage people from making new housing purchases, which tends to create unemployment among housing contractors and in the lumber industry. They also discourage purchases financed by loans—new cars, boats, and second homes. Potential buyers decide whether to purchase by comparing the monthly payment with their monthly income. The higher the interest rate, the higher the monthly payment. And the higher the monthly payment, the higher the probability that growing numbers of consumers will decide that they cannot afford to borrow. This, in turn, creates unemployment, especially in industries such as housing, boat building, and construction.

Because high rates discourage investment, they also hurt the industries that supply businesses—the contractors who construct new plants, the machine tool makers, and those who build heavy trucks and farm equipment. Unemployment in these industries increases as well.

Effects of Deficits on Trade

For the reasons discussed above, interest rates will tend to rise when the federal government runs a large deficit, but savings won't respond very much or very quickly. (Indeed they may fall if inflation is growing as a result.) If there is no additional supply of savings, interest rates will rise and borrowers will be squeezed out of the market. With the rise of international capital markets, this traditional form of crowding out is less common. Instead of borrowing from domestic sources, many companies are now borrowing directly in the Euromarket or they have their foreign subsidiaries raise their capital abroad. Individual Americans generally do not borrow abroad directly. But they do so indirectly when European and Japanese banks come to this country and make loans here, as well as when foreign investors buy American mortgages from federal agencies and mortgage bankers. The federal government itself also borrows abroad when, for example, foreigners buy Treasury bonds.

During most of the 20th century, foreign lending to Americans has been less than American investments in foreign countries. Hence, the U.S. became a creditor nation. However, as the budget deficit has come to consume a large fraction of the domestic supply of savings, there has been an increased need to tap foreign sources of credit in order to satisfy overall credit demands. In order to attract these foreign savings to the U.S., domestic interest rates must be above the rates foreigners can earn elsewhere.

Higher interest rates, however, are not the only cause of this recent surge of foreign capital into our country. Some foreigners feel that the U.S. has the best long-term economic prospects, while others fear that property in their own country might be confiscated or devalued. Consequently, they want to get their capital out of their own country and into the U.S., which is generally considered to be a "safe haven." Some of this capital comes in the form of "direct investment"—purchases of such items as stocks and real estate. The rest comes as loans—for example, purchases of U.S. Treasury bills and bonds.

This foreign money is, in effect, extra money for our economy. It tends to promote U.S. economic activity and keep interest rates from rising even farther and faster. The bad news is that direct investments cause a stream of dividends and other income to flow out of the United States, and loans from foreigners must eventually be repaid, with interest. If the foreign funds are invested productively, paying the interest will not be too much of a burden. But if the money is used to finance government deficits, consumer loans for luxury purchases, and mergers and acquisitions among large corporations, those payments to foreigners will reduce American living standards. Thus, many people view with alarm the fact that more capital now appears to be flowing into the United States than American firms and individuals are investing abroad.

There are other problems as well. Our high interest rates tend to draw lending to our governments, companies, and individuals by people holding their money in yen, marks, pounds, and other foreign currencies. To make dollar-denominated investments, they need to convert these currencies into dollars. With so many people buying dollars and selling foreign currencies, the value of the dollar increased approximately 40% between 1981 and 1985 relative to those currencies. This made goods produced in other countries (our imports) cheaper in the U.S. and made U.S. products more expensive in other countries, thereby hampering our exports.

While the trade deficit is affected by many factors other than exchange rates, most experts agree that the strong dollar significantly increased the deficit in 1981–1985. Even though the dollar has recently declined significantly, especially against the mark and yen, the U.S. trade deficit has not yet begun to show any major improvement. This is because it takes time for a declining dollar to have a noticeable impact on the size of the trade deficit and because the dollar has not declined so much against the currencies of many of our trade competitors.

Americans are now buying more Japanese cars, more Korean textiles, and more vacations in Mexico. Our trading partners, meanwhile, are purchasing fewer U.S. cars, comput-

TABLE 1.9
U.S. MERCHANDISE TRADE BALANCE
($ Billions)

1960	4.9	1977	−31.0	1982	−36.4
1965	5.0	1978	−33.0	1983	−67.0
1970	2.6	1979	−27.5	1984	−112.5
1975	8.9	1980	−25.4	1985	−122.1
1976	−9.4	1981	−28.0	1986	−144.3

ers, and shoes and more from their own companies and from other countries. Businesses respond like people. American manufacturers start buying foreign steel. People with construction contracts in Africa buy their construction machinery from a Japanese competitor, not Caterpillar Tractor. The sum of all these decisions by individuals and firms is the U.S. trade deficit.

What does this mean in jobs? Each U.S. worker on average produces $45,000 in goods or services. If we assume $45,000 of production means about one American job, then Americans lost over 8 million jobs because of imports in 1986. But we gained nearly 5 million jobs because we sell to other countries. The difference—over three million jobs—is the employment cost of the trade deficit. Those jobs are from companies losing out in the export markets, like Caterpillar's laid-off employees, and hundreds of thousands of laid-off auto, steel, and textile workers who lost their jobs because of rising imports.

More on Deficits and Interest Rates

It seems logical that if the government tries to increase its borrowing and nothing else changes, interest rates would tend to rise. That is the view of most economists, along with most of our national political, labor, and business leaders. But not everyone agrees with this analysis.

Interest rates are affected by many different factors. One of the most important is how our economy is performing. When the economy is booming, everybody wants to borrow. Consumers are confident that their incomes will be rising so they are more willing to borrow; businesses need more inventory and are confident they can sell more if they invest in new plants and equipment so they are willing to borrow. Thus, interest rates usually rise in times of economic recovery precisely because people are more willing to take on additional debt when times are good. Under these conditions, high interest rates do not seem to discourage borrowing. On the contrary, they are a sign that the desire to borrow is strong.

During a recession, the reverse is true. Business and consumers are afraid to borrow, and rates tend to fall. Under these conditions, falling rates do not stimulate anyone's desire to borrow. On the contrary, falling rates are a symptom of a shrinking demand for borrowed funds.

Interest rates are also influenced by expectations of inflation. Generally speaking, lenders seek a rate of return that will yield a rate of return that is higher than the expected rate of inflation. If lenders expect stable prices, they may be willing to lend money at 3%, as people did in the 1950s. But if they expect inflation to be 10%, they will need an interest rate of 13% to get the same 3% "real" return after inflation. And if the rate of inflation appears volatile and unpredictable, lenders may demand even higher rates—a so-called "risk premium"—to compensate for the uncertainty.

Because of these and other factors, no one expects changes in interest rates to be determined solely by any one factor, such as the size of the deficit. In other words, an increase in the deficit may be accompanied by a decline in interest rates if inflation falls in the meantime. This is precisely what happened during 1986. Nevertheless, even though interest rates fell while the deficit was increasing, this would not invalidate the claim that deficits affect interest rates. If the deficit had been smaller, interest rates might have been even lower. Although there is no way of conducting an experiment to prove this point—for example, we cannot have a rerun of 1986, leaving everything the same except for the deficit—economists can create statistical models that attempt to show how the economy would behave under different conditions. These models generally indicate that higher deficits mean higher interest rates, but there will never be a way to prove conclusively that the models are accurate or what would have happened differently in 1986 if the deficit had been lower.

Table 1.10 shows the relationship between two key measures of interest rates. The first column is the interest rate on 91–day Treasury bills, which the Treasury issues regularly to finance the deficit. This is also approximately the same as the rate that banks pay on certificates of deposit. Other rates (e.g., bank loans) are higher because they involve more risk and administrative costs for the banks. These rates, which are what borrowers actually pay, are known as "nominal" interest rates. The second column shows the "real" rate of interest, defined as the difference between the inflation rate and the nominal interest rate. It represents the lender's actual gain in purchasing power.

TABLE 1.10
REAL AND NOMINAL INTEREST RATES

	Nominal Interest Rate on 91 Day T-Bills	Real Interest Rate on 91 Day T-Bills
1970	6.46	.96
1971	4.35	.95
1972	4.07	.67
1973	7.04	− 1.76
1974	7.89	− 4.31
1975	5.84	− 1.16
1976	4.99	.19
1977	5.27	− 1.54
1978	7.22	− 1.78
1979	10.04	− 3.26
1980	11.51	− .89
1981	14.03	5.13
1982	10.69	6.79
1983	8.63	4.83
1984	9.58	5.58
1985	7.48	3.68
1986	5.98	4.88

As we can see, while the nominal interest rates have fallen dramatically since 1981, real interest rates have declined much more slowly, and in some years have not declined at all. In 1984 for example, nominal rates were well below levels of earlier years, yet those who lend money were getting much better real returns in 1983 and 1984 than just about any time in our history. Those real returns have declined somewhat in 1985 and 1986, but they are still quite high in historical terms. Of course, this does not prove that high real rates are caused by the government's deficits, but it is certainly consistent with that theory.

Summary: Deficits are Important

- They increase the national debt.
  - —Higher debt causes higher federal interest expenses, making it more difficult to balance the budget in future years.
  - —Higher debt must ultimately force either higher taxes, cutbacks in federal spending other than interest, or both.
  - —Higher debt causes bigger drains on the American economy to pay interest to people and institutions in other countries.
- They tend to drive up interest rates.
  - —Higher interest rates move private money from the young, the poor and the middle class to the older and richer segments of society.
  - —Higher interest rates discourage business investment needed for economic growth.
  - —Higher interest rates encourage foreigners to lend us money, making the dollar more valuable, which worsens our balance of trade and costs some Americans their jobs.

But just because deficits have harmful effects doesn't mean anything will be, or should be, done about them. Both tax increases (discussed in Chapter 3) and spending cuts (discussed in Chapter 4) inflict pain and damage on substantial portions of our population. And, just as important, there is little agreement among politicians, economists, and average citizens as to the most appropriate way to approach the task of deficit reduction.

GETTING OUT FROM UNDER FEDERAL DEFICITS AND DEBT

Repudiation

It is not easy for a government, particularly a stable one, to escape the burdens that its debt creates for its citizens and for its economy. Occasionally, after a revolution, a government will repudiate its debt. However, this is surprisingly rare, primarily because the new leaders recognize that lenders are not likely to extend new loans to a country that refuses to honor its old loans. It would be almost unthinkable for a country like the United States to repudiate its debt. Politically, there would be massive problems when American citizens discovered that their Treasury bonds have been rendered worthless by a repudiation decree. Economically, a government that had just repudiated its debt could hardly expect to go back to those same citizens and ask them to lend more money so that the government could continue running deficits.

Yet the repudiation concept could gain adherents as new generations of Americans become increasingly angered by the immense debt burdens they inherited from prior generations. While direct repudiation of national debt along the lines portrayed in Chapter 1 is unlikely, governments can (and some do) try to reduce their debt burden via inflation.

Inflation

Inflation is one of the most effective, and frequently used, ways of reducing the burden of debt. Consider the case of a

30-year old couple with income of $35,000. This couple might have a $65,000 home mortgage debt, a $5,000 auto loan, $3,000 of credit card debt, and (what they don't see but must shoulder through taxes) a $20,000 share of the federal debt. All told, their debt is $93,000. Merely paying the interest would cost them approximately $10,000, or nearly a third of their income.

But what if the government quickly expanded the money supply, in effect printing more money, adding one new dollar for each old one? This would eventually cause adjustments in wages and prices which would be about equal, so on that account, they wouldn't gain or lose from the ensuing inflation. However, they would now have income of $70,000, and paying off their debt would become less burdensome. With a $70,000 income, their debt would represent a little more than a year's wages. Before inflation, when their income was only $35,000, the debt would have equaled more than two and a half years of income. This simple example illustrates why inflation is the ally of the debtor and the enemy of the creditor.

As the federal government goes deeper and deeper in debt, many fear that deliberate inflation will become an increasingly attractive option. It reduces the debt burden without all the negative political consequences of repudiation. However, unlike direct repudiation, increased inflation penalizes all creditors and savers, not just those who lent money to the government. Any creditor who had lent money at a fixed rate of interest for a long term would be a loser because he could not adjust the interest rate to compensate for the higher inflation.

Government can create additional money in complex ways, mainly by regulating banks and by purchasing and selling securities through the Federal Reserve system. But no matter what technical devices it uses, one thing remains unchanged: inflation occurs when the supply of money increases more rapidly than the supply of goods and services. Some nations, most recently Argentina, Brazil, and Israel, have deliberately generated inflation, partly to cut the burdens of their domestic debt. This results in rapid price increases—sometimes at triple- or quadruple-digit rates. Thus far, the United States has avoided such hyperinflation. Inflation has rarely been more than 10% a year. In the last several years, annual price inflation has been under 5% and less than 2% in 1986.

Inflation has many nasty side effects, and not just for creditors. As prices spiral, some people can't get their wages increased fast enough to keep up. People with fixed incomes, such as private pension plan retirees whose benefits are not indexed to the rate of inflation, are particularly hard hit.

But the worst effects of inflation appear when people come to expect increasing rates of inflation. They tend to spend their money quickly because they know that houses, art, precious metals and other durables will gain in value while money will lose value. This tends to drive up prices even faster. Interest rates also tend to rise as people avoid lending money for long periods unless they are confident that their return will be enough to cover reduced purchasing power. Thus, economic efficiency, investment, and the long term health of the economy can all be damaged by an inflationary spiral.

Growth

Some people believe that the most promising approach to closing the deficit gap is economic growth. They argue that vigorous, sustained economic expansion will tend to increase revenues faster than spending, thereby steadily decreasing the size of the budget deficit, both absolutely and as a percentage of GNP. Conversely, they argue that significant spending cuts or legislated revenue increases, whatever their intended purpose, would actually end up expanding the budget deficit by retarding economic growth. Critics of the "growth" solution say that we've tried it over the past five years and it hasn't worked. One of the longest economic expansions in U.S. history has left us with annual deficits between $150 and $200 billion, with no end in sight. The real choice, they say, is between explicit deficit-reduction measures and perpetual deficits.

Repudiation, inflation, and growth represent three approaches to the federal deficit that do not rely on spending cuts or tax increases. Chapters 3 and 4 will discuss options for doing what these three approaches rule out—namely, raising taxes and cutting spending programs. While these options differ significantly, they all rest on the assumption that repudiation, inflation, and growth are either ineffective or unacceptable as deficit-reduction strategies.

APPROACHES TO DEFICIT-REDUCTION

Most economists and politicians believe that the consequences of continued deficits in the hundreds of billions of dollars, even during periods of economic recovery, are unacceptable. They agree, therefore, that the deficit should be placed on a downward path. But there is disagreement over whether the end point should be a surplus, a balanced budget, or merely a smaller deficit. There are also disagreements over the speed with which this target should be reached. The following are some of the principal approaches to deficit-reduction.

End Deficits and Run Surpluses to Retire Existing Debt

This approach considers the impact of debt to be so serious as to merit not only balanced budgets but also sufficient surpluses so that the outstanding federal debt can be repaid as quickly as possible. This path would obviously result in a reduction of the debt. But substantial surpluses could slow economic growth by reducing demand for goods below our capacity to produce them. Tax revenues used to pay off debt would draw funds from taxpayers who would otherwise spend most of these funds in ways that would stimulate overall economic activity. Repayment of debt would be made to persons and institutions (e.g., foreigners, financial institutions, pension funds, wealthy individuals) who would typically not use much of the money for consumption in the U.S.

One possible partial solution to this problem is to finance repayment of the debt out of accumulated wealth rather than incomes. Taxes with this effect include estate and gift taxes and a possible new tax based upon wealth. Another possible solution is to run the big surpluses only when the economy is overheating—that is, when taking money out of the economy helps long-term growth.

Perpetually Balanced Budgets

Balanced budgets mandated by Constitutional amendment would end the deficit problem in the future without addressing the problem of accumulated past debt. Debt would remain constant in absolute terms. But as the nation's GNP increased as a result of real growth and inflation, the percentage of GNP consumed by debt and annual interest payments would decline steadily until, after several generations, it became negligible. This path would reduce the burden of debt and interest payments over time.

A Balanced Budget Over the Business Cycle

This view argues that the budget should be balanced during the course of the business cycle, with deficits in recessions counterbalanced by surpluses during recoveries. If the deficit followed this path, there would be surpluses in years of higher-than-average growth, such as 1984, and those surpluses would increase as the recovery continued. There are substantial practical problems with this approach, however. It assumes economists can predict recession and recovery and that political leaders will be willing to run surpluses rather than distribute them through tax relief and higher spending.

A Full Employment Balance

Another approach would seek a balanced budget, but only when the economy is at "full employment." That is, there would be no deficit or surplus when the economy was performing at full capacity. But deficits would be acceptable as long as unemployment exceeded the rate defined as "full." One problem with this approach is that there is no agreement as to what now constitutes full employment, nor is there likely to be. Another problem is that this approach implies deficits in most years, hence a steadily rising national debt.

The "Tolerable" Deficit

This approach rests on the premise that there is a point (measured as a percentage of GNP) where deficits are small enough to be tolerable. At that point, the detrimental effects of deficits (e.g., higher interest rates) become small enough so that they neither cause massive economic dislocations nor sow the seeds of subsequent recessions or depressed growth patterns. The number most often mentioned in association with this concept is that deficits should not exceed 2% of GNP.

Establishing a tolerable deficit target does not involve a threshold under which everything is good and nothing is bad and over which nothing is good and everything is bad. Instead, it is a continuum along several dimensions. For example, if the tolerable deficit is set at 2.1% rather than 2.0% of GNP, interest rates would be slightly higher, the dollar somewhat stronger, exports somewhat less, imports somewhat greater, and so forth. On the other hand, taxes would be lower, expenditures higher, or both.

Factors that might be taken into consideration in defining a "tolerable deficit" could include historical deficit patterns, deficit levels in other countries, one's preferences for spending and tax levels, and as many other factors as there are effects of deficits. But as was the case with the "full employment" approach, the definition of the "tolerable" deficit is deeply contested and vulnerable to continued shifts in the balance of political power.

Constant Debt Burden

Another approach would be to freeze the national debt as a percentage of GNP. This would allow total debt to rise at the same rate as GNP. For example, if GNP is expected to rise by approximately 2.5% in 1988, outstanding government debt, which now totals nearly \$2.4 trillion, would also be allowed to rise by 2.5%, or approximately \$65 billion. Given stable interest rates, such a course would also freeze interest costs as a percent of GNP. While freezing the problems associated with debt, however, this policy would not solve problems associated with persistent deficits.

Attempting to Achieve a Particular Quantity of Investment

Another approach to deciding how much federal debt can be tolerated as a percentage of GNP is to set investment targets, estimate future supplies of domestic savings and foreign capital, and see how much "room" is available for the federal deficit.

The choice of a target investment level would be somewhat arbitrary. Because the years 1977 through 1979 were relatively good ones, the average investment (business and housing combined) level of those years, 17.4% of GNP, could be taken as the target. Saving by households, businesses, and state and local governments has been quite stable as a combined total, averaging about 18.3% of GNP between 1977 and 1985. With zero financing by foreigners, this would suggest "room" for a federal deficit of 0.9% of GNP, or about \$40 billion in 1988. To make room for a larger deficit, it would be necessary, given a fixed investment target, either to increase business, personal, and local government savings or to borrow from abroad.

However, the natural economic force of higher interest rates cannot cause the necessary change in savings while preserving the target level of investment. As noted earlier, savings behavior tends to be much more insensitive to interest rate changes than business investment and consumer borrowing to purchase housing. Thus, ways would have to be found to encourage more saving by consumers and businesses while not increasing interest rates. One way to do that would be through changes in tax laws.

Gramm-Rudman-Hollings Deficits

In late 1985, Congress passed the Gramm-Rudman-Hollings bill and, after legal and political controversy, revised it in 1987.

This important piece of legislation—and the arguments for and against it—will be discussed in greater detail in the following chapter and also in Chapter 5. But at this point, it should be mentioned that it tries to force Congress and the Administration to put the deficit on a trajectory that will lead to a balanced budget in 1993, by mandating "automatic" spending cuts in the event that Congress and the President cannot agree on deficit-reduction packages that meet yearly deficit targets between now and 1993.

Summary of Longer-Term Deficit Approaches

The table below summarizes the long-term approaches to deficits. (The "quantity of investment" approach is not included because its consequences depend on unpredictable facts about the performance of the U.S. economy.)

TABLE 1.11

SUMMARY OF ALTERNATIVE DEFICIT STRATEGIES

| Strategy | Budget Condition in time of: | | | Change in Debt over time: | |
	Recession	Normal Growth	Over-heating	Absolute Amount	As % of GNP
Pay off Debt	Surplus or Balanced	Surplus	Surplus	Reduced	Reduce
Balanced Budget	Balanced	Balanced	Balanced or Surplus	Stable	Reduce
Balance Over Cycle	Deficit	Balanced	Surplus	Stable	Reduce
Full Employment	Deficit	Deficit*	Balanced* or Surplus	Increased	Probably Reduced
Tolerable Deficit	Deficit	Deficit	Deficit	Increased	Depends on Plan
Stable Burden	Deficit	Deficit	Deficit	Increased	Stable
Gramm-Rudman-Hollings	Moving** to Balance	Moving** to Balance	Moving** to Balance	Increased**	Reduced

*If a normally growing economy is assumed not to have full employment, this concept allows a deficit during normal growth.
**Until 1993.

The Glide Path

Advocates of these various patterns realize that large deficits are built into current policies and that massive changes in spending and/or taxes would be required to eliminate the entire deficit in one year. Thus, they seek typically a deficit reduction path that moves the budget towards the eventual deficit goal over a number of years.

Many consider this gradual ("glide path") approach appropriate because most of the deficit-correction measures have deficit impacts that increase from year to year. For example, holding down Social Security costs by subtracting 1% from cost-of-living increase saves about 1% in the first year, 2% in the second, and so forth. Reducing the rate of increase in defense spending compounds in this way also, as do the effects of many other measures.

CHAPTER 2

The Budget Process

How much money the government decides to spend, borrow, and collect in taxes has a major impact on living standards and the long-term health of the economy. In view of the significance of these decisions, it is important to understand not only how government expenditures, taxes, and deficits affect the economy, but also how Congress and the President make these crucial decisions.

Table 2.1 presents a page from President Reagan's proposed 1987 defense budget, which was submitted to Congress on February 5, 1986. According to the spending category called total "budget authority," the defense budget declined from $294.6 billion in 1985 to $286.1 billion in 1986. Yet despite this apparent $8.5 billion decline, another item in the defense budget called "total outlays," rose from $252.7 billion to $265.8 billion, for a total increase of just over $13 billion.

What's going on here? Was defense spending declining by $8 billion or rising by $13 billion? Which number is correct? Or to put it differently, which number gives a better overall picture of the size and direction of defense spending? Can defense spending increase at the same time that the defense budget is being cut?

To understand how Congress makes budget decisions, it is important to be able to answer these questions as well as to understand the difference between such technical budget terms as outlays and budget authority. And to track the progress of something as crucial as the defense budget through the House

TABLE 2.1

NATIONAL DEFENSE

(Functional code 050; $ Millions)

Major missions and programs	1985 actual	1986 estimate	1987 estimate	1988 estimate	1989 estimate
BUDGET AUTHORITY					
Department of Defense-Military:					
Military personal	67,773	67,672	74,203	75,430	76,119
Operation and maintenance	77,803	74,851	85,773	90,890	97,281
Procurement	96,842	92,611	95,777	102,400	112,030
Research, developmment, test and evaluation	31,327	33,736	41,930	42,108	41,303
Military construction	5,517	5,281	6,743	8,999	8,982
Family Housing	2,890	2,801	3,396	4,076	4,515
Revolving funds and other	5,182	2,123	1,270	1,707	1,637
Offsetting receipts:					
Existing law	−532	−713	−843	−840	−873
Proposed legislation			100		
Allowances: Civilian pay raises			716	1,732	2,766
Allowances: Military pay pay raises and benefits			2,611	5,929	9,664
Allowances: Other legislation (proposed)		50	−77	−32	74
Subtotal, Department of Defense-Military	286,802	278,412	311,600	332,400	353,500
Atomic energy defense activities	7,325	7,232	8,230	8,720	9,300
Defense-related activities	528	471	510	452	429
Total, budget authority	294,656	286,115	320,340	341,572	363,229
OUTLAYS					
Department of Defense-Military:					
Military personal	67,842	71,438	73,610	74,842	75,548
Operation and maintenance	72,348	74,137	80,872	81,023	87,163
Procurement	70,381	75,702	76,708	81,243	88,881
Research, developmment, test and evaluation	27,103	28,702	31,618	36,649	38,447
Military construction	4,260	4,545	4,592	5,473	6,590
Family Housing	2,642	2,446	2,491	3,010	3,506
Revolving funds and other	1,325	2,143	1,847	1,851	1,852
Offsetting receipts:					
Existing law	−532	−713	−843	−840	−873
Proposed legislation			100		
Allowances: Civilian pay raises			704	1,668	2,668
Allowances: Military pay pay raises and benefits			2,568	5,873	9,600
Allowances: Other legislation (proposed)		25	−2	−92	−83
Subtotal, Department of Defense-Military	245,371	258,425	274,265	290,700	313,300
Atomic energy defense activities	7,098	7,152	7,708	8,400	9,000
Defense-related activities: Existing Law	279	250	515	29	−18
Proposed legislation			−250		
Subtotal, Defense-related activities	279	250	265	29	−18
Total, outlays	252,748	265,827	282,238	299,129	322,282

of Representatives, it is important to understand the different
roles played in the budget process by the House Budget
Committee, the House Armed Services Committee, and the
Defense Subcommittee of the House Appropriations Committee. All three are involved in determining how much money
the U.S. will spend for defense. But each plays a distinct role
in shaping the defense budget. Understanding these differences, knowing how Congress and the President go about the
business of making a budget, and understanding some of the
important concepts used by them during their deliberations
should help to clarify who is responsible for what and how
government officials carry out their crucial budget-making
duties.

THE BUDGET PROCESS

Article I section 9 of the Constitution states that "no money
shall be drawn from the Treasury, but in consequence of
appropriations made by law; and a regular statement and
account of the receipts and expenditures of all public money
shall be published from time to time." The Constitution also
states that Congress shall have the power to levy taxes and
print money. But aside from granting those three powers to
the Congress, the Constitution makes no explicit mention of a
federal government budget or the budget process. Because of
the Constitution's silence, Congress and the President have
been free to devise their own rules and procedures.

Although the budget process is extraordinarily long and
tedious, at first glance there is no reason why it should be so
complex. During the course of the year, Congress could simply
exercise its constitutional authority to appropriate money and
levy taxes. At the end of the year, it could tote up how much
it spent and how much it raised in taxes. The difference would
be the deficit or surplus. If Congress does not like the results,
it could resolve to change next year's spending and tax policies.

It all sounds simple, but in fact, managing the federal budget is one of the most complicated and least understood government functions. In broad general terms, since 1976, the budget process has consisted of four distinct steps. Beginning in 1986, a fifth important step was added. Those five steps are as follows:

1. The President drafts a budget for all the government's activities and submits it to Congress.

2. The House and Senate Budget Committees evaluate the President's budget and either amend it or, as has been the case recently, devise a totally different, competing budget outline.

3. Authorizing committees in the House and Senate determine which programs will be eligible to spend government money.

4. The House and Senate Appropriations Committees determine precisely how much money each program will be able to spend during the upcoming year.

5. If the projected deficit exceeds a specified level, a "sequestration" process is begun in which spending is cut and the deficit reduced to the required level.

The President's Budget

The budget process officially begins in early January when the President sends his budget to Congress. The budget represents the President's financial plan for the country. In it, he specifies how much money the government expects to receive in taxes, the total amount of spending planned for the year, and the resulting deficit or surplus. In addition to these aggregate figures, the President's budget details precisely how much money the Administration wants to spend on every federal program.

These detailed spending recommendations are presented in a variety of formats so that Congress can evaluate the President's recommendations from different perspectives. One presentation shows how much money the Administration is requesting for every part of the federal government, such as the Department of Defense, the Department of Agriculture, the Federal Communications Commission, and the National Security Council.

This format shows how the different government bureaucracies are planning to slice up the spending pie. But it does not provide a very clear picture of how much money is being spent on specific government functions such as national defense, education, and law enforcement. A large number of law enforcement operations, for example, are administered by the Department of Justice. But the Department of Treasury has control over some law enforcement operations such as the Secret Service and the Bureau of Alcohol, Tobacco and Firearms. Similarly, most national defense spending is done by the Department of Defense, but the development and production of nuclear weapons, which is also part of the defense budget, comes under the purview of the Department of Energy.

In view of this bureaucratic division of labor, telling Congress how much money each agency will be spending next year does not necessarily provide much information about the President's specific spending priorities. To provide Congress with this information, the President is required by law to present his budget in terms of 19 different functional spending categories—defense, foreign aid, education, housing, social security, agriculture, veterans affairs, and others. By examining this version of the budget, Congress can see how much money the President is recommending for each type of government service, independent of which part of the bureaucracy will actually be running the program.

These two different ways of looking at the budget are compared in Table 2.2 and Table 2.3. The data come from President Reagan's FY88 budget, which he submitted to Congress on January 5, 1987. The numbers show that while the President proposed $289.3 billion for the Department of Defense, this actually understates the total amount of proposed defense spending. As the figures for the National Defense function reveal, the President's total defense spending proposal amounted to $297.6 billion, or approximately $8 billion more than the military portion of the Department of Defense budget. Similarly, the figures indicate that while the Department of

TABLE 2.2
PROPOSED OUTLAYS BY AGENCY, 1988

Agency	Amount ($ Billions)
Legislative Branch	2.2
The Judiciary	1.4
Funds Appropriated to the President	13.4
Agriculture	50.7
Commerce	2.3
Defense-Military	289.3
Defense-Civil	22.1
Education	14.7
Energy	10.2
Health and Human Services	146.8
Social Security	214.5
Housing and Urban Development	13.9
Interior	4.4
Justice	5.8
Labor	25.4
State	3.6
Transportation	24.6
Treasury	187.3

TABLE 2.3
PROPOSED OUTLAYS BY FUNCTION, 1988

National Defense	297.6
International Affairs	15.2
General Science, Space, and Technology	11.4
Energy	3.3
Natural Resources and Environment	14.2
Agriculture	26.3
Commerce and Housing Credit	2.5
Transportation	25.5
Community and Regional Development	5.5
Education, Training, Employment	28.4
Health	38.9
Medicare	73.0
Income Security	124.8
Social Security	219.4
Veterans Benefits and Services	27.2
Administration of Justice	9.2
General Government	7.5
General Purpose Fiscal Assistance	1.5
Net Interest	136.0

Justice was budgeted for $5.8 billion, the President was proposing to spend $9.2 billion for the law enforcement operations known as the "Administration of Justice."

Both perspectives are useful in evaluating the federal government's spending priorities. But neither indicates whether a particular item is slated for a spending increase or decrease. And more importantly, even if an item is scheduled for an absolute spending increase, Congress still would not know whether the scheduled increase is sufficient to provide the same level of services and benefits as it agreed to provide last year. Without additional information, in other words, a Presidential proposal that looks like a spending increase could actually turn out to entail a reduction in services or benefits.

Therefore, to evaluate the President's proposals, as well as to help in devising its own alternatives, Congress requires the President to present a "current services" budget which shows how much money each function and agency would need in order to provide the same level of services and benefits as last year. By comparing the current services budget with the Administration's actual spending recommendations, Congress can determine more precisely which programs are being given new responsibilities and which are shrinking.

The Congressional Budget

Although the President is required to submit a budget, Congress is under no legal obligation even to vote on the Administration's recommendations, let alone enact them into law. If it chooses, Congress can totally ignore the President's budget and craft a radically different spending plan. Of course, with the constitutional system of checks and balances, the President can veto any spending and tax measures passed by Congress. So in fact, all budget decisions represent a compromise between the President's priorities and those of the Congress. But the existence of these compromises does not change the fact that the ultimate constitutional authority for deciding how much money will be spent for each program rests with Congress.

The work of devising the Congressional version of the federal government budget starts in the House and Senate Budget Committees. Working separately, each Committee drafts a budget resolution which spells out the total amount of tax revenues it wants the government to collect, how much money it wants the government to spend, and the resulting deficit or surplus. In addition to presenting these spending and revenue totals, the budget resolution specifies how much money Congress wants to allocate for each government function such as national defense, interest on the debt, the administration of justice, and so on.

After the House Budget Committee completes its review of the President's proposals and finishes drafting its revised version of the federal government budget, the entire House of Representatives votes on whether to approve, disapprove, or modify the budget resolution proposed by its Budget Committee. The Senate follows a similar procedure when it evaluates the resolution drafted by its Budget Committee.

During the debate on the budget resolution, Members of Congress can vote to approve it without changes, or they can drastically revise the proposed budget. But revisions and amendments cannot call solely for spending more money on a particular function. Instead, if a member wants to propose a spending increase for one function, he must also specify how that additional spending will be financed. Does he propose to increase the deficit? Is he suggesting that taxes be raised? Or does he want to reduce spending on some other function? Any of these three options is perfectly legal. But the important point is that during the debate on the budget resolution, Members cannot propose additional spending without also calling for higher taxes, a higher deficit, or less spending on some other function.

After both chambers pass their respective versions of the Budget Resolution, a conference between members of the House and Senate Budget Committees is convened to iron out any differences. This compromise version becomes the official Congressional budget. It is this document, and not the President's budget, that guides Congress's remaining spending and tax decisions.

What is the legal status and function of the budget resolution? In the first place, because the final product is termed a resolution, and not a law, it does not need the President's signature. Although the resolution is frequently worked out in close consultation with the White House, Congress is not legally required to get the President's blessing for its budgetary handiwork. And in fact, as Table 2.4 shows, the Congressional version of the federal budget frequently differs quite substantially from the President's initial proposal.

In the FY88 budget, for example, the President, House, and Senate all reached similar conclusions about the appropriate level of total spending, revenues, and deficits. But the spending priorities of both the House and Senate were significantly different than those of the President. In particular, the House and Senate both called for much lower rates of defense spending and higher funding levels for domestic programs. The President, on the other hand, recommended just the opposite—more for defense and less for domestic programs. Nevertheless, in both the House, Senate and Administration versions of the budget, spending for all categories—defense and domestic—was slated to rise above its 1987 levels.

TABLE 2.4

ADMINISTRATION, HOUSE, AND SENATE BUDGET BLUEPRINTS
($ Billions)

	House Budget Resolution	**Senate Budget Resolution**	**Administration Budget Proposal**
Budget Authority	1142.2	1158.2	1142.2
Total Outlays	1038.5	1039.8	1024.4
Total Revenues	930.9	932.0	916.6
Deficit	107.6	107.8	107.8
Defense	288.7	289.0	312.0
Interest	139.1	145.4	139.1
Social Security	259.1	256.8	256.8
Other Domestic	455.4	467.0	434.4

Second, although the budget resolution must specify the precise deficit that will result from the spending and revenue decisions, until recently, there was no limit on the size of the deficit that could be recommended. Deficits exceeding $200 billion were perfectly legal. And in fact, the largest deficit ever specified in a Congressional Budget Resolution was $181.2 billion for FY85. In late 1985, however, Congress passed the Balanced Budget and Deficit Control Act of 1985, more popularly known as Gramm-Rudman-Hollings. That law established a maximum permissible deficit for fiscal years 1986 to 1991. In September of 1987, this law was amended to provide maximum permissible deficits until 1993. Under the terms of this law, neither the President nor Congress can propose deficits that exceed the specified levels.

Third, the Budget Resolution sets out a series of targets for spending, revenues, and the deficit. But, until recently, when Congress actually got down to deciding how much money to spend, it was under no obligation to hit those targets, or even to aim at them. Between 1980 to 1986, for example, the actual deficit exceeded the level specified in the budget resolution by an average of $48 billion. A portion of these errors is due to the fact that Congress spent more and taxed less than it said it would when it drafted the budget resolution. Congress, in other words, simply did not enact the specific tax and spending legislation that was needed to implement the resolution and achieve the deficit targets.

But even larger discrepancies were caused by economic forecasting errors. In trying to decide what the appropriate level of revenues and expenditures should be, Congress needs to have some estimate of the health of the economy. Raising taxes in the midst of a recession may prolong the downturn and actually increase the deficit. Similarly, a healthy, rapidly growing economy will mean higher tax collections, lower spending for such items as unemployment compensation, and a smaller deficit. Although Congress cannot possibly predict the precise state of next year's economy, neither can it calculate next year's projected spending, revenues, and deficit without making some assumptions about the level of unemployment, inflation, interest rates, business profits, and economic growth. Estimated deficits will be lower if the Congressional forecast specifies rapid growth, higher if the forecast indicates a recession.

Since neither Congress nor the President is willing to go on record as forecasting a recession or even moderately slow growth, the estimates of spending and revenues are generally based on what turn out to be overly-optimistic economic forecasts. But because it consistently overestimates economic growth, Congress also consistently underestimates the size of the actual deficit. The largest forecasting error occurred in 1982, when a failure to foresee the steepest recession since the 1929 Great Depression meant that the actual deficit was three times greater than the deficit called for in the budget resolution. In that year, economic forecasting errors were responsible for a $76 billion underestimate of the size of the actual deficit.

Finally, unlike the President's budget which specifies precisely how much money will go to each agency and federal program, the Congressional budget resolution only specifies how much money will be spent on broad, general categories. The resolution talks in terms of general functions like national defense, not specific programs like nuclear air craft carriers or the Strategic Defense Initiative. The actual work of determining how much money will be spent on specific programs is not done by the Budget Committee but by the authorizing and appropriations committees.

Authorizing Committees

Before the government can spend any money, Congress has to pass legislation establishing a program and creating its rules, regulations, responsibilities, and eligibility requirements. Drafting this so-called "authorizing legislation" is done by the various authorizing committees in Congress. Examples of authorizing committees in the House of Representatives include the Banking, Finance and Urban Affairs Committee which has jurisdiction over federal housing programs; the Armed Services Committee which is concerned with deciding which military programs should be included in the defense budget; the Education and Labor Committee which deals with such items as worker training programs and student loan programs; the Public Works Committee which has jurisdiction over highway, mass transit, and water programs; and the Ways and Means Committee, which in addition to writing tax legislation, sets the eligibility requirements for Social Security, Medicare, Medicaid, unemployment compensation, and a variety of welfare programs.

For example, when it drafts Social Security legislation, the Ways and Means Committee establishes rules specifying how many years someone has to work in order to receive retirement benefits. Other items that might be included in authorizing legislation are whether retirees should receive annual cost of living adjustments, the minimum retirement age at which benefits will be paid, and the maximum age at which the government will pay benefits to the children of deceased workers. Similarly, the Armed Services Committee decides whether the Navy should acquire a new nuclear aircraft carrier, whether the U.S. should deploy the MX missile, how much money should be spent on spare parts and ammunition, and whether to allow research and development to proceed on the Strategic Defense Initiative.

In addition to specifying the rules that will govern each federal program, the authorizing committees determine the maximum amount of money that can be spent on a particular program. Some programs are known as entitlements because anyone who meets the eligibility requirements is entitled to receive a check from the federal government. Examples of entitlement programs are Social Security, Medicare, and farm price supports. Because they are set up as entitlements, Congress does not establish maximum spending levels for these programs. Instead, after the eligibility requirements are spelled out, a typical authorizing bill would contain a section declaring that Congress authorizes the appropriation of "such sums as may be necessary." For non-entitlement programs, spending is limited by the actual amount of money authorized and appropriated by Congress. Since these programs do not entail an open-ended commitment to spend whatever money is needed to meet the demand for that particular government service, typical authorizing language for these programs states, "there is hereby authorized to be appropriated the sum of $X million for Fiscal Year 1987 for carrying out the purposes of this act."

The Appropriations Process

Just because a particular program passed muster with an authorizing committee does not mean that it will find its way into the final federal budget or that it will have as much money to spend as the authorizing bill specified. Determining which programs will be funded and how much money they will actually be allowed to spend is the role of the House and Senate Appropriations Committees. During the course of their annual deliberations, the Appropriations Committees are expected to draft 13 separate appropriations bills. In effect, the appropriations bills specify precisely how much money will be put in the checking account of each federal program listed in the appropriations bills.

What do the appropriations committees appropriate? A reasonable answer would be "money." In fact, this is not quite technically correct. The appropriations committees actually appropriate something known as "Budget Authority," or the authority for a particular agency to sign contracts, write checks, and spend money. For example, before the Navy can acquire a nuclear aircraft carrier, Congress first has to authorize its acquisition and then appropriate the approximately $4 billion of budget authority needed to purchase the carrier.

However, once this amount is appropriated, next year's spending for that aircraft carrier will not necessarily total $4 billion. It takes several years to build an aircraft carrier. During that time, the Department of Defense will be sending regular progress payments to the shipbuilding company so that the company can pay the weekly wages of its workers and for the electronics equipment, steel, and other parts that go into an aircraft carrier.

The monies that are actually spent in any particular year are known as "outlays." Outlays, and not budget authority, are used in calculating the deficit, which is technically defined as the difference between outlays and revenues. Thus, even though Congress may appropriate $4 billion of budget authority for an aircraft carrier, the immediate impact on the deficit will generally be much less. The precise effect depends on the amount of outlays that are associated with that appropriation in any particular year.

In fact, because not all budget authority is spent in the year in which it is appropriated, the actual level of government spending and deficits in one year are the result of appropriations decisions made during the current year as well as earlier years. For FY88, for example, President Reagan called for new budget authority totalling $1,142.2 billion. The Administration estimated, however, that only $731.8 billion of that new budget authority would be spent—would appear as outlays—during FY88. The remainder would be spent in later fiscal years. The Administration also estimated that $292.5 billion of outlays would occur during FY88 as a result of budget authority that had been appropriated earlier. Consequently, total outlays in 1988 were estimated to be $1,024.3 billion, consisting of the $731.8 billion from this year's budget authority and $292.5 billion from earlier budget authority.

This distinction between budget authority and outlays helps explain why it is so difficult to slow the growth of federal spending. As Table 2.1 indicated, even though defense budget authority for FY86 was being cut, actual outlays continued rising as projects that were funded earlier moved toward completion.

This distinction also explains why Congress can cut the defense budget, in the sense of reducing budget authority available for national defense, at the same time that actual defense outlays continue growing. Unless Congress actually cancels earlier appropriations and voids contracts that were already signed—a step that is politically difficult and unpopular because it means throwing defense workers out of existing jobs—it can take several years for a reduction in appropriations to produce a reduction in outlays. The sheer momentum of previously appropriated budget authority virtually guarantees that spending will continue rising for several years after the growth of budget authority is slowed or halted. In fact, according to the Administration, by the end of FY88 the federal government will have approximately $1,256.9 billion of unspent budget authority.

A second reason it is so difficult to cut spending has to do with the relative controllability of certain government spending programs. Although no spending can occur unless Congress first appropriates money, annual Congressional appropriations only cover a relatively small portion of total government spending. During FY86, for example, the 13 appropriations bills only provided $535 billion of budget authority. Another $725.8 billion of budget authority was available even though funds for these programs were not included in annual appropriations bills. For the most part, these programs consist of interest on the national debt and entitlements.

The bill appropriating funds to pay interest on the national debt was passed in 1847. It provides a permanent appropriation of budget authority so that the Treasury Department can pay whatever amount is needed to service the national debt. Although it is highly unlikely that Congress would move in this direction, the fact remains that if it wanted to, Congress could always repeal that 1847 legislation and refuse to appropriate all the funds needed to pay interest. In fact, as Chapter 1 suggested, if the debt and annual interest payments continues growing, and as more of the debt is held by foreigners, U.S. citizens could in theory decide that they do not want to pay the taxes or give up the public services so that government funds will be available for foreign creditors. In fact, a number of Latin American governments have taken similar steps recently, arguing that their countries' need for growth and higher standards of living must take precedence over the interest payments owed to foreign creditors, in this case, primarily commercial banks.

Entitlements are another category of relatively uncontroll-able spending. When Congress passes authorizing legislation establishing an entitlement program, it also passes an appro-priations bill that allows the program to spend whatever funds are needed to pay benefits to anyone who is entitled to receive them. If Congress wants to reduce the cost of these entitle-ments, it must change the provisions of the authorizing legis-lation establishing the eligibility requirements or the size of the benefit. But as long as the authorizing legislation remains unchanged, the ability of Congress to control the outlays associated with these programs is relatively limited.

The distinction between budget authority and outlays, cou-pled with the fact that outlays for certain programs are not easily controllable via annual appropriations, means that the Appropriations part of the budget process actually has much less maneuvering room to hold down outlays—and hence the deficit in any particular year—than is generally recognized. For example, according to data released by the Office of Management and Budget (OMB), total outlays for FY86 were $989.8 billion. Approximately $402.6 billion of outlays were for entitlement programs such as Social Security, student loans, unemployment compensation, and federal employees' retirement. Another $136 billion went to pay interest on the national debt and $25.8 billion was spent on farm price support programs.

Together, these various items totalled $564.1 billion. An-other $181.3 billion of outlays was the result of previously appropriated budget authority, leading to a grand total of $745.4 billion of spending that was not immediately controll-able through annual appropriations. The remainder—the con-rollable portion of outlays—therefore amounted to just under $245 billion, or approximately 25% of total government spend-ing.

Gramm-Rudman and Sequestration

In late 1985, Congress added a fifth step to the budget process when it declared that the budget deficit should be eliminated by 1991. To accomplish this, Congress mandated that between 1986 and 1991 neither the President's budget nor the Congressional budget resolution would be permitted to recommend a deficit higher than the following amounts:

($ Billions)					
1986	1987	1988	1989	1990	1991
171	108	108	72	36	0

In September 1987, Congress revised Gramm-Rudman-Hollings by postponing the mandatory balanced budget until 1993 and revising the targets for the intervening years upwards, as follows:

1988	1989	1990	1991	1992	1993
144	136	100	64	28	0

Unlike previous years, when the budget resolution targets were ignored or missed with relative impunity, Congress was determined to use Gramm-Rudman-Hollings to ensure that the targets would be hit, no matter what policies the budget committees, authorizing committees, or appropriations committees actually enacted during the course of the annual budget cycle. With this in mind, Congress devised an across-the-board spending reduction process known as "sequestration."

For FY 1989 and beyond, the sequestration process begins in mid-August, when the Congressional Budget Office (CBO) and the Office of Management and Budget (OMB) prepare their estimates of the deficit for the fiscal year scheduled to begin two months later on October 1. This estimate takes into account all the authorization and appropriations bills actually enacted into law from the beginning of the year until the time deficit projection is made. If the OMB determines that the appropriations, authorization, and tax changes enacted by Congress since the start of the budget cycle will not be sufficient to get the deficit to within $10 billion of its maximum permissible level for that year, the sequestration spending reduction procedure is invoked.

According to this procedure, CBO and OMB prepare a list of spending reductions designed to ensure that the final deficit will, in fact, not exceed the maximum permissible amount. In preparing their lists of spending reductions, they have to follow several rules and guidelines.

First, the outlay reductions have to be divided evenly between defense and nondefense programs. In other words, 50% of the spending cuts have to come from defense; the other 50% have to come from the other programs in the budget. Second, Social Security, veterans compensation and pensions, interest on the national debt and a number of low income programs such as food stamps and child nutrition are exempt from any sequestration reductions. Finally, the deficit reduction has to be accomplished only via spending reductions, not through tax increases.

After CBO and OMB prepare their independent estimates of the required spending reductions, the president issues an order putting into effect the reductions as calculated by OMB.

After receiving the President's August sequestration order, Congress and the President have approximately six weeks in which to adopt deficit-reduction steps sufficient to bring the deficit for that year down to the specified ceiling. In mid-October, CBO and OMB repeat their sequestration procedure, with estimates updated to reflect any legislation that may have been enacted since August. If the Gramm-Rudman-Hollings targets still have not been met, the budget cuts calculated by OMB automatically go into effect.

The revised version of Gramm-Rudman-Hollings received its first test in late 1987. After the 508–point stock market collapse on October 19, Congress and the Administration began negotiations on a package designed to reduce the deficit by at least $23 billion, the amount of government spending subject to automatic cuts (''sequestration'') for fiscal year 1988. After almost a month of talks, agreement was reached on the outlines of spending cuts and tax increases sufficient to avoid sequestration. Both defense and non-defense spending were reduced, and taxes were raised by $9 billion. Although the difficult task of translating this general agreement into specific legislation lay ahead, Gramm-Rudman-Hollings appeared to have achieved its intended effect—forcing political leaders with sharply conflicting priorities to strike a compromise that would move the government toward deficit-reduction.

Legislation for fiscal 1988 would represent only the first step on the long and arduous road to a balanced budget. In the years to come, political leaders will have to consider further compromises and a wider range of deficit-reduction options. Chapters 3 and 4 sketch the current revenue and spending policies of our government and examine some important deficit-reduction possibilities in each category.

CHAPTER 3

Raising Revenues

This chapter discusses recent trends in federal revenues and various options for increasing them.

Where the Government Gets its Money

Table 3.1 shows how the federal government expects to raise approximately $1,138 billion of revenues in FY 1991. In the absence of any major revisions of the tax laws, most of the revenues are projected to come from taxes on individuals. The individual income tax is expected to be the government's biggest source of revenues, raising 44% of the total. The Social Security (FICA) tax will be the next biggest money maker, raising slightly more than one-third of all federal revenues. This tax is paid in equal amounts by both employees and employers. Taxes on corporate profits are expected to generate

TABLE 3.1
PROJECTED FEDERAL RECEIPTS BY SOURCE, FY1991

	Amount ($ Billions)	Percent
Individual Income	502	45
Corporate Income	151	12
Social Insurance	411	36
Excise	33	3
Miscellaneous	51	4

13% of all federal revenues. Finally, miscellaneous receipts such as customs revenues, inheritance taxes, and excise taxes will generate the remaining 4%.

How High are Taxes Now?

Both the amount of money the federal government raises as well as the ways in which it raises those revenues have changed significantly over the past twenty years. Moreover, they will continue changing dramatically between now and 1992, even if no revisions are made in current tax laws.

Measured in terms of real 1982 dollars—that is, after removing the effects of inflation from the data—total federal government revenues increased from $461.9 billion in 1967 to $541.0 billion in 1977 and $642.0 billion in 1981. By 1986, the amount of inflation-adjusted revenues had increased still further to $673.0 billion. Thus, between 1967 and 1986, real federal government revenues, and hence the government's ability to spend without going into debt, increased by slightly more than $210 billion. Federal spending, however, increased much more, rising from $488 billion to $866 billion, or by just under $400 billion. Hence, the current deficits.

Another widely accepted way of measuring the level of taxation is to compare tax receipts to the total output of the economy—gross national product or GNP. As Table 3.2 indicates, even though real federal government revenues rose considerably since 1967, federal taxes as a percent of GNP remained relatively constant. For example, federal government receipts amounted to 17.7% of GNP in 1967. Twenty years later in 1986, after several recessions, the war in Viet Nam, four Presidents, and numerous changes in the tax code, federal government receipts had risen to only 18.4% of GNP. By 1991, they are expected to rise still further to 19.4%. However, that level is still below the peak reached on several earlier occasions, although it is somewhat higher than the typical level for this period.

The table suggests that 20% of GNP may be the maximum

TABLE 3.2
TAX RECEIPTS AS A PERCENT OF GNP

1967	18.7	1980	19.4
1968	18.0	1981	20.1
1969	20.1	1982	19.7
1970	19.5	1983	18.1
1971	17.7	1984	18.1
1972	18.0	1985	18.6
1973	18.0	1986	18.4
1974	18.6	1987	19.3
1975	18.3	1988	19.0
1976	17.6	1989	18.9
1977	18.4	1990	19.3
1978	18.4	1991	19.4
1979	18.9		

level of federal taxation that most voters are willing to tolerate these days. Some people therefore believe that the way to deal with federal government finances is to establish a ceiling on the level of federal taxes relative to GNP. However, with spending currently at 23.8% of GNP, setting the revenue ceiling at 20% of GNP would entail either substantial deficits or substantial spending reductions. Voters, in other words, would either have to accept fewer government services or be willing to continue borrowing in order to finance the services they want. Establishing a higher ceiling, on the other hand, would allow the government to finance higher spending levels without incurring larger deficits. But precisely because it would reduce pressures on Congress to cut spending, many advocates of a revenue ceiling insist that only a low ceiling makes political and economic sense. The goal, they claim, is to cut spending, not to raise taxes.

Some state governments currently have constitutional limits governing the maximum level of taxes or spending relative to the size of their total economies. But many opponents argue that such limits would be impractical for the federal government because it must be able to deal with expensive crises, such as major wars.

The Burden of Federal Taxes

Nobody likes paying taxes, for several reasons. First, they are involuntary and people resent not having any choice in the matter. Second, not everyone approves of all the different programs the federal government supports with those tax dollars. Third, and perhaps most crucially, practically any tax system will seem unfair to someone—particularly those who pay more under the current system than they would under some alternative system.

Over the past twenty years, the way in which the federal government raises revenue has changed dramaticaly, and will continue changing during the next six years, as Table 3.1 indicates.

Perhaps the most noticeable change is the decline in the corporate income tax burden coupled with the rise in the share of revenues generated by the Social Security payroll tax, which is divided about equally between individuals and corporations. In 1967, for example, slightly more than one out of five tax dollars was raised by the corporate income tax. By 1986, that share had fallen to one dollar in twelve. As a share of GNP, corporate tax collections also declined, falling from 4.3% in 1967 to only 1.5% in 1986. During that same period, Social Security's share of total tax collections rose from one in five dollars to more than one in three. And as a share of GNP, these taxes rose from 4.1% in 1967 to 6.8% in 1986.

Between now and 1991, Social Security's share of the total

TABLE 3.3
**PERCENT OF TOTAL FEDERAL REVENUES RAISED
BY TYPE OF TAX**

	FY67	FY77	FY81	FY86	FY91
Individual Income Tax	41.3	44.3	47.7	45.4	45.0
Corporate Income Taxes	22.8	15.4	10.2	8.2	11.7
Social Security Taxes	21.9	29.9	30.5	36.9	36.5
Excise Taxes	9.2	4.9	6.8	4.3	2.9
Miscellaneous Receipts	14.0	10.4	11.6	9.5	3.9

tax burden is not expected to change appreciably. However, corporate tax payments are expected to rise to 11.6% of all federal tax payments. At that point they will constitute approximately 2.3% of GNP. The main reason for this increase is the 1986 tax reform bill (to be discussed in more detail below) which shifted some of the tax burden from individuals to corporations.

Taxes, Tax Reform, and Economic Efficiency

Taxes affect the economy by reducing both the total amount of money available for private consumption and investment and the way in which people actually consume and invest. When people give a little extra to charity because it is deductible, or take out a second mortgage on their house so that they can receive a tax deduction on the interest, or buy tax-exempt bonds so they do not have to pay taxes on that income, and when corporations purchase equipment to take advantage of "accelerated depreciation" or buy other corporations for their "tax loss carry-forward," the overall shape of our economy is changed to some extent—and not necessarily in ways that increase efficiency and productivity. Hence the way in which the government might decide to raise additional revenues as part of some deficit reduction package could have major impacts on the health of the economy, as well as on the economic well-being of different groups in society.

When tax rates are high, the tax code has the greatest potential for distorting economic decision-making and reducing economic efficiency. In our income tax system, the key variable is what taxpayers pay on an added dollar of income or don't pay by claiming an added dollar of deductions (the so-called marginal rate).

Until recently, someone with taxable income of about $50,000 had a marginal rate of approximately 43%. This means that for every $100 of extra income, that individual had to pay an extra $43 of federal income taxes. Since that individual could only keep $57 out of every $100 of extra income, there were strong incentives to reduce the tax "bite" by investing in tax shelters and to avoid reporting income by working "off the books."

All too frequently, investment and work decisions that were not necessarily good for the economy turned out to be best from the individual taxpayer's point of view. Taxpayers had strong incentives for making investment decisions on the basis of how much in taxes that investment would allow them to avoid, not on the basis of whether that investment made sense from a free market, profit and loss perspective. The result, many people claimed, was that too much taxpayer energy went into avoiding taxes and not enough into improving the economy.

Besides encouraging people to make decisions that did not necessarily improve efficiency and productivity, the combination of high marginal tax rates and numerous tax loopholes created an impression that the tax code was unfair. It allowed two people with the same income to pay different amounts of taxes. For example, by investing heavily in tax shelters, one taxpayer could cut his tax bill while a second person who was making the same number of different investments—but ones that did not generate such large deductions—would wind up paying more in taxes.

To eliminate these inefficiencies and inequities, Congress and the Administration agreed on a far-reaching tax overhaul package in 1986. To guide the drafting of that bill, three principles were established. First, President Reagan insisted that the bill be revenue neutral. It could not, over a period of years, generate any more—or less—revenue than the old system. Second, reductions in marginal tax rates would be "paid for" by eliminating tax loopholes. In other words, the extra revenues generated by eliminating various deductions and credits would be returned to taxpayers in the form of lower marginal rates. In effect, therefore, people who had been using large numbers of loopholes would now be paying more so that other people who had been paying their fair share all along could now start paying less. A final principle was that a larger portion of the tax burden should be transferred from individuals to corporations. This was to be accomplished by eliminating a large number of corporate tax deductions and using some of those revenues to pay for individual rate reduction.

The tax bill that was finally passed by Congress and signed into law by the President, The Tax Reform Act of 1986, established two marginal tax brackets for individuals. As of 1988, individuals with taxable incomes below $17,850 and families with incomes below $29,750 were subject to a 15% marginal rate. A 28% rate was levied on incomes above these levels. In addition, due to certain technical factors, individuals whose incomes were between $43,150 and $100,480 (or $71,900 and $192,930 for families of four) will actually be facing a 33% marginal rate while the wealthiest pay only 28%. Thus, under the new code, the top marginal rate for the highest income taxpayers will be 28%, down from the 50% rate prevailing before tax reform and the 70% rate that was in existence before 1981. In addition, the top corporate rate was reduced from 46% to 34%.

Although supporters claim that these reforms will make the tax system both more equitable and efficient, the fact that the bill was revenue neutral means that Congress passed up an initial opportunity to kill two birds with one stone—reform the tax code and reduce the deficit. Moreover, by closing some of the most widely used loopholes in order to pay for lower tax rates, tax reform eliminated some of the most obvious tax changes that could be enacted in the name of deficit reduction. Nevertheless, even in the post-tax reform era, there are still several ways that more money could be raised from the new tax system.

Raising Income Tax Revenues

The most obvious way to increase income tax revenues is simply to raise tax rates. For example, a "surcharge" might be imposed on all individual and corporate taxpayers. Under this system, taxpayers would calculate their taxes as they do now and then add another five or ten percent to their tax bills. (A similar result could be achieved by raising existing tax rates across the board.) A second possible option is to add a new

33% bracket that would pertain only to the wealthiest individuals and families. A final option is to allow the corporate tax rate to decline to only 35% or 40%. Even these rates would represent a significant reduction from the 46% rate that was in effect before tax reform, but it would not be as low as the 34% rate that was included in the original tax reform legislation.

Proponents of these changes note that with any of these alternatives, most taxpayers would still experience substantial rate reductions, albeit not as large as they originally expected. In addition, supporters argue that a surcharge, higher rates, or a new bracket would raise a significant amount of revenue quickly and with very few administrative complications. Finally, supporters note that adding a 33% bracket for upper income taxpayers would ensure that the wealthiest do not pay at a lower rate than the middle class.

Opponents say that unless low income taxpayers were exempted from the surcharge, many of them would be paying a higher marginal rate under the new system than under the old one. This is unfair. Opponents also argue that adding a new tax bracket for upper income taxpayers would be unfair, and possibly unwise. The 1986 Tax Reform Act was a carefully-crafted compromise in which loopholes were closed in return for lower marginal tax rates. Raising rates paid by the wealthiest taxpayers would violate that bargain. Moreover, if higher rates increased public pressure for restoring some recently-eliminated loopholes, many of the inequities and inefficiencies that were purged from the code would soon start reappearing. This should be avoided at all costs. Finally, corporations have already accepted a larger share of the total tax burden and very shortly they will be paying more than one-eighth of all federal tax receipts. If the U.S. economy is to regain competitiveness, business must have enough cash to be able to boost investments for new plant and equipment. Any further increases in the corporate tax burden could decrease the ability of corporations to make these vital investments.

As an alternative to adjusting marginal tax rates and imposing surcharges, additional income tax revenues could also be generated by eliminating some of the deductions (or loopholes, depending on your point of view) that were left intact by the 1986 tax reform bill. This approach would still raise substantial amounts of revenue, but it would do so by enacting less dramatic piecemeal changes in the tax code. As might be expected, such changes tend to affect relatively smaller numbers of people (whose taxes would be raised). Therefore, the changes are both easier for Congress to adopt (because of the smaller number of persons affected) and harder (because those affected argue they are being unfairly singled out for higher taxes when the burden should be spread more evenly).

Such changes could include eliminating deductions for such items as state and local income and property taxes, certain charitable contributions, and taxing certain benefits provided by employers ranging from free parking to generous health plans and personal legal services.

For example one of the most costly deductions still on the books allows taxpayers who itemize to deduct all state and local income and property taxes from the income they report on their federal returns. Repealing that deduction would ensure that taxpayers in low-tax states do not subsidize taxpayers in high- tax states. Also since state and local taxes pay for purely local services such as schools, fire departments and police, the federal government has no business subsidizing these items, either directly through government spending programs or indirectly through the income tax code. Opponents argue, however, that federal budget cuts are already shifting an increasing share of the spending burden onto state and local governments. If the federal government is going to give added responsibility to the states, it should not also make it more difficult for states to pay for these services.

Consumption Taxes

In reality, there are three things governments can tax—income, consumption, and assets. Currently, the federal system relies almost totally on taxing income. If amending the newly-revised income tax code is not feasible, or if the revisions would not raise enough revenue to eliminate the deficit, then the U.S. might need to start thinking about ways to increase taxes on assets or consumption.

Serious consideration has been given in some quarters to the idea of national consumption taxes. By taxing income, the United States makes people pay taxes on their total income, including that portion used for savings and investment. The argument is that if the federal government taxed money only when people spent it for consumption, people would tend to increase their savings and investment. This, in turn, would help reduce interest rates and make it easier to finance long-run economic growth.

Excise Taxes. There are a number of ways to tax consumption. The most familiar and widespread is the way the states do it now—a sales tax calculated as a certain percentage of the purchase price. Although it is not widely recognized, the federal government currently imposes a number of sales taxes. These federal sales taxes are known as excise taxes. When you purchase tires for your car, or when you buy cigarettes, gasoline, wine, beer, and liquor, or when you make a long distance phone call or buy an airline ticket, a federal excise tax is added to the price of the item.

Ways of raising more money from the existing excise tax system include increasing the tax rate on items already subject to the tax or, alternately, imposing the tax on a wider array of goods and services. One of the most widely heard suggestions is to raise the tax rate on items that are considered harmful, such as alcohol and tobacco. Opponents of these so-called "sin taxes" argue that they are a greater burden on poor people than on wealthier families and that this is unfair. They also note that higher taxes may discourage people from using these substances, but if so, they won't raise much money, particularly if some of the production goes underground and escapes taxation altogether.

Another proposal that has been seriously advocated from time to time is some sort of excise tax on energy. The most comprehensive approach would tax the value of all energy consumed in the country, irrespective of whether it is derived from imported oil, domestic coal, natural gas, etc. Such a tax is viewed as likely to promote energy conservation and to reduce American reliance on foreign oil supplies. A narrower approach would be just to tax imported oil. In addition to raising substantial revenues that could go toward deficit reduction, a tax on imported oil would also help domestic energy producers by allowing them to charge higher prices for their oil. This would help alleviate some of the oil industry's financial difficulties. However, some political leaders, especially in the northeast, object to a tax on imported oil because it would increase energy prices in the northeastern states (which gets oil from abroad) while all the benefits would go to domestic oil producers in other parts of the country.

Another variant on the energy tax idea is to levy much higher taxes on gasoline, as many European nations now do. Besides raising money, such a tax would encourage Americans to drive smaller, more fuel-efficient cars and discourage people from selecting jobs and residences that require long commutes. Sudden imposition of such an increase would, however, create some hardships for persons now committed to larger cars and for persons, especially in the West, who must travel long distances for business and personal reasons. Also, it would not provide any financial relief to the domestic oil industry and, by encouraging conservation and reducing consumption, might actually worsen their financial plight.

Value Added Tax (VAT). Excise taxes are collected at the cash register and are therefore, considered to be highly visible. For example, with a 5% excise tax, a $100 item actually costs $105. The sales receipt clearly notes that the price is $100 and that a $5 tax has been added to that price, bringing the total cost to the customer to $105. A value-added tax (VAT), by contrast, is imposed at each stage of the production process. Like a 5% excise tax, a 5% VAT will bring the price of a $100 item to $105 at the point of final sale, but the tax need not be specified on the sales slip.

With a VAT, the purchase price is listed as $105 and the customer pays precisely that amount. Because the cost of the tax is hidden, some people argue that once a VAT is imposed, politicians will be tempted to raise the rates in the hope that the voters won't notice the increase. However, most European governments as well as Japan rely on a VAT to supplement their income tax system, and their voters always seem to know when the politicians are changing the rate.

While excise taxes are only levied on a small number of items, supporters of a VAT would generally apply it to the same items that are currently subject to most states' sales taxes. In other words, the VAT would be paid by everyone every time a purchase is made. One consequence is that a VAT would be particularly onerous for poor and middle income people. Even though everyone is taxed at the same rate, poor people tend to spend a greater proportion of their income than wealthier individuals. As a result, a larger percentage of their income would be subject to the tax. In technical terms, this means that the tax is "regressive."

One way to solve this problem is to link the VAT to the income tax system. Under this arrangement, low and moderate income people would be able to reduce their income tax by at least a portion of whatever amount they paid as a VAT. This tax credit would be phased out for middle income families and would not be available at all for upper income taxpayers. Alternatively, a wide range of necessities such as food and medicine—items which make up the bulk of purchases among poorer people—could, as in Western Europe, be exempted from the VAT altogether. At the same time, a higher VAT rate could be imposed on luxury goods consumed primarily by the rich.

Better Enforcement

Even after tax reform, many Americans still believe that other Americans don't pay their fair share of taxes. Part of this feeling stems from a belief that the remaining loopholes still allow too many inequities. For example, if your employer pays the cost of your health insurance, the value of those insurance premiums does not count as taxable income. This means that individuals whose employers pay the cost of their health insurance are in a better financial position than those workers whose employers do not provide health insurance and who, therefore, must use after-tax income to pay their health insurance premiums.

However, much of the concern is directed to those who avoid taxes through illegal conduct. Examples are not reporting income received in cash (e.g., tips, some cab fares, money paid to plumbers and electricians in cash), keeping two sets of books in small business, and keeping income off the books by barter arrangements. Other concerns relate to questionable deductions, such as overvalued contributions to charity.

Some estimate that the revenue lost through tax evasion exceeds $100 billion a year. However, this evasion won't be easy to stop. Much of it comes from activities that are already clearly illegal, such as drugs and prostitution. Since society can't successfully prevent these activities, it is unlikely that government can monitor them well enough to collect taxes on them.

Some forms of evasion could be prevented, however, by much stricter IRS enforcement of existing tax laws. One example is more complete auditing of tips that are charged to credit cards. Another would be to require a better accounting of dividend and interest payments made by banks and other corporations. There is, of course, considerable public resistance to the added reporting and increased paperwork, as well as to the higher budgets IRS would need to use this information effectively.

Social Security Taxes—A Special Case

While payroll taxes for Social Security raise considerable revenue, they aren't considered a likely candidate for increase. All of the revenues from these taxes go to special funds used for paying Social Security benefits and certain health care costs for persons over 65. (As we will see in the next chapter, although these revenues are set aside, they do affect the overall budget deficit figure.) Laws already passed will cause these taxes to increase further over the next decade. Revenues from Social Security taxes will likely be sufficient to pay retirement benefits until well into the next century. Paying for health benefits is another matter, as discussed in the next chapter.

Summing Up

As this chapter shows, there is no shortage of ways for the federal government to reduce the deficit by raising taxes. The problem, of course, is that many Americans don't want to raise taxes.

For those willing to consider this strategy, Table 3.4 gives an indication of how much money could be raised by the various options.

Some tax law changes, such as rate increases, could be made immediately. Others, such as a VAT, would probably be

TABLE 3.4

CHOICES FOR RAISING TAXES

The Tax Choices	**What They Raise** **($ Billions)**
CONSUMPTION TAXES	
Sales or Value-Added Tax	
For each 1% (no exemptions)	22
Exempt food, housing and medical expenses	13
Energy Taxes	
Oil import fee of $5 per barrel	8
Gasoline tax of 25 cents per gallon	23
Tax all energy consumption at 5%	17
Excise Taxes	
Raise cigarette tax to 32 cents per pack	3
Increase beer and wine taxes	6
Extend telephone long distance tax	3
INCOME TAX CHANGES	
Surcharge on Individual Income (5 Percent)	25
Surcharge on Corporate Income (5 Percent)	8
Add a 33 Percent Bracket for Individuals	11
Set Top Corporate Tax Rate at 35%	3
Eliminate Deductibility of State and Local Taxes	27

phased in over several years. To put these on a comparable basis, the table below shows how much various measures would raise in FY 1991. (Recall that the deficit for that year, assuming Congress makes no changes in existing tax or spending programs, is currently projected to be $165 billion but could be well over $200 billion if the economy enters a recession in the next year or so.)

CHAPTER 4

Cutting Spending

This chapter discusses recent trends in federal spending and the various spending reduction options.

Where Federal Money Goes

Table 4.1 shows the principal ways the federal government spends money and how the federal government's spending priorities have changed during the last twenty years.

In 1967, national defense accounted for just under 50% of total government spending while entitlements—Social Security, Medicare, Medicaid, military and civil service pensions, aid to families with dependent children, and agricultural price supports—accounted for slightly more than 25%. By 1981,

TABLE 4.1

OUTLAYS FOR MAJOR SPENDING CATEGORIES
($ Billions)

	1967	1977	1981	1986	1991
National Defense	71.4	97.2	157.5	273.4	333.0
Entitlements	46.0	199.2	323.5	457.3	618.0
Social Security and Medicare	24.5	103.9	179.3	270.9	392.0
Other Domestic	40.1	104.5	167.7	170.3	215.0
Net Interest	10.3	29.9	68.7	136.0	179.0
Total	157.5	409.2	678.2	989.8	1280.0

Note: Totals do not add due to certain technical factors affecting the definition of total outlays.

73

national defense had fallen to less than 25% of total government outlays while the entitlement share had risen to approximately 50%.

These relative shares did not change dramatically between 1981 and 1986, despite a 50% increase in total government spending and a heated debate about the appropriate role for the government in the economy. Nor are current budget policies expected to change these relative shares between now and 1991. National defense will continue to absorb slightly more than 25% of outlays while entitlements consume approximately 50%.

The most dramatic changes since 1981 occurred in the two categories labeled "other domestic" and "net interest." Despite a 50% increase in total federal outlays between 1981 and 1986, spending for other domestic programs—which includes virtually every other federal program such as housing, energy conservation, running the Congress and national parks, salaries for federal workers, operations of the FBI, etc.—barely increased in dollar terms and fell sharply as a share of total government spending. Meanwhile, interest payments on the federal debt more than doubled. Interest payments now consume almost 15% of all outlays, up from 6% in 1967 and 10% as recently as 1981. Assuming Congress meets the Gramm-Rudman deficit targets, the share of total outlays consumed by net interest is expected to fall back to the neighborhood of 12% by 1991.

Budget Cutting and Sacred Cows

Some people argue that various parts of the budget should be exempt from spending cuts. These programs are the so-called sacred cows—items that some people believe should be spared at all cost. While there may be good reasons for exempting a particular program, the fact is that as more programs are declared off-limits, the remaining programs will be subject to even deeper cuts.

For example, suppose Congress wanted to reduce FY 1991 spending by $100 billion, with tax increases and savings in interest costs bearing the rest of the budget balancing burden. As Table 4.2 indicates, the size of the cuts inflicted on the remaining eligible programs varies directly with the number and size of the programs exempted from cuts.

TABLE 4.2

**PERCENTAGE CUTS IN OUTLAYS NEEDED
TO REDUCE SPENDING BY $100 BILLION IN FY 1991**

Exempt These Items	and Cut This Much
Nothing	7.9%
Social Security (except medical)	9.6%
National Defense	10.6%
National Defense and Social Security	14.2%

Uncontrollable Interest Costs

Almost every week the Treasury Department borrows additional funds from the public so that the government can finance its current deficit and repay—or roll-over—earlier borrowings that are coming due. The government does not have much choice about this borrowing. If it does not borrow additional funds, it will literally run out of cash. Social security checks could not be mailed (or would bounce if they were mailed), and the government would be unable to pay its employees and contractors.

When the government borrows from the public, it signs a contract promising to pay a specified rate of interest and to repay the principal on a certain date. Most people believe these contracts should be honored. Otherwise, people would stop lending money to the government and government spending would grind to a halt.

Creditors are free to lend their money to the government or to anyone else they choose, so federal officials must pay whatever the market rate of interest happens to be at that moment. They cannot dictate the interest rate, which is set in the market based on the supply and demand for loanable funds. Nor can they control how much is being borrowed. That decision is made by Congress in the course of its revenue and spending deliberations. Since the Treasury Department cannot control either the interest rate or the amount it has to borrow, total interest payments on the federal debt are officially designated as an "uncontrollable" federal expense.

Of course, interest costs can be controlled—but only by controlling the amount of borrowing, which means reducing the deficit. Saving money on interest payments, therefore, is not a direct route to deficit reduction, but rather a consequence of reducing the deficit via other spending and revenue decisions. For example, putting federal finances on a path that would cut $100 billion in FY 1991 from federal programs would also reduce interest costs by about $35 billion. Hence the total deficit reduction in that year would be $135 billion.

Trust Funds

About a third of the federal budget is financed with trust funds. These funds contain money that is earmarked for particular uses and "held in trust," separate from other government revenues. One example is the highway trust fund. The federal government imposes a tax on gasoline and diesel fuel. The proceeds are used for the construction and maintenance of certain federal highways. Another trust fund raises money from an excise tax levied on airline tickets. This trust fund finances airport construction and modernization.

Over long periods of time, these trust funds do not generate deficits since their receipts and expenditures are generally in balance. Nevertheless, reducing trust fund outlays also reduces the overall deficit, at least in the short run. By cutting trust fund expenditures, total government spending for that year is reduced. And since the deficit is the difference between total spending and total revenues, irrespective of whether that spending is financed from trust funds or some other source, the deficit is also be reduced.

On the other hand, cutting spending in a trust fund like the one for highways or airports may not have much of a long-term impact on the deficit. If spending is cut, highway and airport users could make a strong case that the taxes going into the trust fund should also be cut. This revenue reduction would increase the aggregate deficit, thereby offsetting any short-term deficit reduction benefits of the spending cuts.

Social Security and Budget Deficits

The Social Security program is the largest trust fund program in the federal budget. One critical issue is whether these programs should be excluded from any deficit reduction package.

"Social Security" actually consists of a number of trust funds, including retirement and disability, related retirement funds for railroad workers and coal miners affected by black lung disease, and a hospital insurance fund for Medicare benefits. According to the authorizing legislation establishing the Social Security program, Social Security tax receipts must be deposited in the various Social Security trust funds. These funds cannot be used for any purpose except to pay benefits to eligible individuals. Since the spending and revenue side of these trust funds are so completely segregated from other federal spending and revenue programs, some people believe that Social Security should not even be discussed in the same breath as the federal deficit.

Despite this legal segregation, however, there is a strong arithmetic link between Social Security and the deficit. In practice, the calculation of total federal receipts, expenditures, and deficits includes the receipts, expenditures, and balance in the Social Security trust fund. In other words, even though Social Security is not a legal component of the federal budget, its surplus or deficit does have a direct bearing on the calculation of the total federal deficit. If Social Security runs a surplus and the rest of the budget is in deficit, the overall deficit is reduced dollar for dollar by the amount of the Social Security surplus. And if the Social Security trust fund has a surplus, it lends the money to the rest of the government, which reduces the amount that has to be borrowed from the general public.

As Table 4.3 indicates, during the next several years, Social

TABLE 4.3
FEDERAL DEFICITS WITH AND WITHOUT SOCIAL SECURITY

Fiscal Year	Including Social Security Surplus	Excluding Social Security Surplus
1986	221	237
1987	148	168
1988 (proj.)	183	221
1989 (proj.)	192	236
1990 (proj.)	176	229
1991 (proj.)	165	227

Security's impact on the deficit is expected to be quite significant. Were it not for the surpluses in the Social Security trust funds, the actual federal deficit would be as much as nearly $70 billion higher. The amount by which other programs would have to be cut would also be increased commensurately. From this arithmetic perspective, therefore, the mere existence of the Social Security trust funds goes a long way toward alleviating the budget cutting pressures faced by the other programs. Consequently, many people argue that Social Security is already making a considerable contribution toward deficit reduction and should be exempt from any additional cuts.

During the late 1970s, it became clear that the revenues of the Social Security system would be inadequate to finance its mounting pension outlays. Many controversial proposals for dealing with this situation were put forward in the early 1980s. In 1983, President Reagan and congressional leaders established a bipartisan task force, which made recommendations for increasing the solvency of the Social Security trust funds. These recommendations were later adopted by Congress. It is generally believed that those tax increases and benefit reductions will ensure the system's solvency until well into the 21st century.

Because the Social Security problem is deemed to be solved and because they fear a political backlash if they reopen the subject, many political leaders do not want to consider budget cutting plans that include Social Security. And in fact, Gramm-Rudman specifically exempts Social Security from any sequestration-ordered spending cuts. Opponents of further Social Security cuts argue that this program is primarily responsible for an extraordinary decline in poverty among the elderly and a rise in their quality of life. They do not want to see these gains reversed or eroded.

But others argue that Social Security is such a large part of the budget that any "balanced" plan for deficit reduction should include at least some restraint on its benefits. They argue that while domestic programs for the poor and the disadvantaged have been slashed during the 1980s, Social Security has been left virtually untouched and its costs have soared. Since it is among the largest and most rapidly growing program in the federal budget, it would be unfair to exclude it from a broad-based package of spending cuts.

There are several ways this restraint could be engineered. For example, since the mid–1930s, when the normal retirement age was first set at 65, and at 62 for early retirement with reduced benefits, the longevity of Americans has increased by more than 10 years. As a result, many more persons live to retirement age, and they live longer after they reach it. For this reason, the most significant cost-saving measure in the Social Security retirement program would be to raise the retirement age.

However, most people agree that it would be unfair to impose these changes in a way that affects people who are nearing retirement. Therefore, any change in the retirement age would probably have to be phased in so that workers within five years of retiring might not be affected at all; those within ten years of retirement might have their retirement date delayed by a matter of months; and the full delay would apply only to new workers. This means that while the long-term cost savings would be substantial, the changes would have very little effect on federal spending and deficits over the next five years, where the concern over closing the deficit is concentrated.

More immediate savings would be possible if the formula for

determining cost of living adjustments, or COLAs, could be adjusted. Currently, benefits are increased every year to reflect changes in the cost of living during the preceding year. The result is that the purchasing power of Social Security benefits remains constant, but at the cost of a constant increase in Social Security outlays, and hence in the size of the federal deficit.

Some people believe that the deficit could be reduced if the COLA formula were changed so that it protected retirees from only a portion of the increased cost of living. For example, the COLA increase could be limited to two-thirds of the cost of living increase. Under this plan, if inflation were 6%, benefits would rise by only 4%. Those who support such a move say Social Security recipients do not need the full cost of living adjustment. They are already sheltered from a portion of the annual cost of living increase because most retirees own their homes and basic household possessions. Hence, changing the COLA formula would not cause them any real hardship. Opponents argue that the change would be unfair and would push hundreds of thousands of retired people below the poverty line. These people clearly need the full cost of living increase, yet this proposal would prevent them from receiving it.

Another approach, frequently advocated in conjunction with a one-year freeze on all federal spending, would be to skip the cost of living adjustment for that year. This would save money in the year the COLA was skipped and in every subsequent year because each year's increase is based on the benefit paid during the prior year. Consequently, a lower benefit in one year has a compound effect over the lifetime of each retiree.

Since inflation is currently not very high, a one year freeze on COLAs would not impose a particularly onerous burden on retirees and yet because of the compounding effect, it would have a significant impact on the deficit. Once again, however, opponents point out that many retirees are currently just above the poverty line. Even a one year suspension of their cost of living adjustment would be an unfair imposition.

In one respect, Social Security's problem is that it is an "entitlement." Anyone who works the requisite number of years and pays taxes into the Social Security trust fund is entitled to receive benefits. Because both rich and poor pay taxes into the Social Security trust funds, rich and poor alike receive benefits. Millionaires get monthly checks just like impoverished retirees. Moreover, the money to finance these benefits is deducted from the paychecks of today's workers—in effect taxing today's rich, poor, and middle class alike to pay benefits, some of which go into the pockets of the rich.

Since millionaires do not depend on Social Security for their retirement income, some people argue that benefits should be reduced or eliminated for those retirees with significant amounts of other income. Under this proposal, changes in the COLA formula, or proposals to skip the COLA, would only effect upper income retirees. Benefits would not be cut for anyone if Social Security is their main source of retirement income. Those opposed to these sorts of changes note that Social Security will not continue to enjoy its strong political support if it is converted into a quasi-welfare program. And without the strong political support of the middle and upper classes, the political consensus for paying such generous benefits to relatively poorer retirees will erode.

Rather than reducing or eliminating Social Security benefits for wealthy retirees, an alternative approach is to increase taxes on Social Security benefits. Under current law, individuals with at least $25,000 of outside income or couples with at least $32,000 of outside income pay income tax on half their Social Security benefits. Some people want to eliminate or reduce these income thresholds so that a larger number of Social Security recipients are required to pay income taxes on their Social Security benefits. Others suggest making 85% or even 100% of Social Security benefits—up from the current 50%—subject to the income tax.

Either option would reduce the after-tax benefits of upper income retirees. And both options would treat Social Security benefits more similar to the way that other pension benefits are treated. And because of other provisions of the income tax code, anyone depending on Social Security for all or most of their retirement income would still receive tax-free Social

Security payments. Consequently, fewer Social Security benefits would go to people who do not need them and yet the universal character of the system would remain unaltered.

Nevertheless, opponents argue that this proposal would still be unfair. The current tax on benefits was enacted as part of the 1983 Social Security reform and financial rescue package. At that time, it was agreed that well-to-do retirees would contribute to the financial solvency of the Social Security system by paying income taxes on a portion of their Social Security benefits. According to the opponents of expanding the tax, it would be wrong to tamper with the 1983 compromise, especially now that Social Security surpluses are beginning to make a major contribution to deficit reduction and the financial solvency of the Social Security system is not in question.

Health Care and Medicare

Medicare provides government-paid health insurance for an estimated 31 million persons who are aged, disabled, or suffering from kidney disease. Medicare Part A pays hospitalization costs for all qualified individuals. It is a mandatory program, financed by a portion of the Social Security payroll tax. Medicare Part B reimburses physicians for "reasonable" charges for all covered services. Most of the cost of the Part B program is financed out of general government revenues; the remainder is financed by monthly premiums—currently $17.90—paid by beneficiaries.

Like Social Security, the hospital insurance part of the program is handled by a trust fund financed by payroll taxes paid by employers and employees. Unlike Social Security, however, this trust fund is not expected to remain solvent through the rest of this century. Experts differ on *when* trouble will occur but not on *whether* it will.

The cause of Medicare's financial problems is not difficult to fathom. As the over–65 population grows, the number of persons eligible for Medicare benefits has been growing more rapidly than the number of active workers paying taxes into the trust fund. In addition, health care costs have been rising faster than other prices, for several reasons. Advances in medical technology are making better care possible, but at a higher cost. And for the past two decades, the system of health care payments has encouraged—indeed, virtually ensured—rapid inflation.

Congress has already taken some steps to control costs, including a new system for limiting how much hospitals can bill the Medicare system each time a patient is admitted for a particular illness. But even though this helps control costs, it will not restore the trust fund's solvency. Consequently, there must be either further cuts in the program, or some of the costs must be shifted to those who get the benefits, or payroll taxes must be raised, or some combination of these measures.

The out-of-hospital coverage (known as Part B) is not funded by payroll taxes. Instead, those who purchase the coverage pay about $17 a month and the federal budget covers the rest—approximately $50 a month for each person enrolled. One way to cut federal spending for this portion of the program would be to reduce the federal government's share by making recipients pay a larger fraction of the Part B costs when they actually receive treatment.

For example, when the Part B program was first established in 1972, premiums financed 50% of the Part B costs. Today, Part B premiums account for only 25% of the program's cost. Increasing the premiums so they would finance 30% of the program's cost would cost recipients only $7 a month, but would generate a significant reduction in the federal government's Medicare outlays. Since the additional premium would only amount to 5% of the average monthly Social Security benefit, supporters argue that this would not be an onerous burden for the elderly. However, some people object to this proposal on the grounds that at least some of the elderly would find the increased premiums burdensome. They would drop Part B coverage and, when they could not pay their doctor bills, locally-financed public hospitals would be forced to absorb the costs of caring for these patients.

Another alternative for reducing health care costs is to

increase the Medicare deductible from $75 to $200. The deductible is the amount that beneficiaries have to pay for services each year before the Medicare program starts making payments. The deductible has only increased twice since 1966, when it was originally set at $50. If the current $75 deductible had been adjusted for past inflation, it would be $175 in 1987.

Supporters note that out of pocket costs under this proposal would increase by only $125 per year per recipient. Potential beneficiaries who do not get sick would not have to pay any additional charge. Also, the poor would not have to pay the added cost since their deductibles are already paid by Medicaid or by state public assistance programs. Opponents argue that even a small increase in out-of-pocket costs could prove burdensome to low income beneficiaries who do not qualify for Medicaid. The added burden might discourage them from seeking needed medical attention until they are extremely ill, at which point the cost of their care would be much higher than if their problems had been diagnosed and treated much earlier.

The federal budget also covers other health care costs. Health benefits are provided to military personnel, merchant seamen, certain veterans, pregnant women, and a variety of other special categories of people. In addition, the federal government sponsors health research and subsidizes the education of doctors, nurses, and other health care specialists.

There is considerable interest in trying to hold down health care costs for everyone, not just the share that is paid from the federal budget. This is not easy. While many people think doctors make too much, they constitute only 9% of all the professionals working in health care. The rest of the health providers—nurses, orderlies, and others—are not generally regarded as overpaid. Furthermore, much of the cost of health care comes from goods sold in regular markets—food, fuel, beds and linen, cotton, and the like. Health care cost controls can also try to squeeze out inefficiency in the system, such as unnecessary tests and excessively long hospital stays. Some people believe that further moves in this direction could cut federal health care spending without damaging patient care; others have their doubts.

National Defense

Because defense constitutes about a fourth of the federal budget, it is difficult to talk about major spending reductions without including defense. But discussions of the defense budget confuse most Americans because they do not have a clear idea either of the way the U.S. spends its defense dollars or of the military capabilities of the United States and its adversaries.

The defense budget is currently divided into the following categories listed in Table 4.4 below.

The defense budget is large—approximately $1,200 a year for every American. These resources buy considerable military capacity: nearly 2.2 million men and women in uniform, approximately one million civilian employees of the armed services, many more civilian employees working for defense contractors, 17 Army divisions, 1,000 Minuteman land-based strategic missiles, 96 attack submarines, 13 aircraft carriers and their supporting vessels, and much more.

Defense costs are determined by three fundamental factors: (1) what, as a nation, we want to accomplish with military force; (2) how efficiently and effectively resources are used to accomplish these missions; and (3) the military capabilities of actual or potential adversaries.

TABLE 4.4

PERCENTAGE DISTRIBUTION OF DEFENSE APPROPRIATIONS, FY 1987

Category	Percent
Military Personnel	26
Operations and Maintenance (including civilian personnel)	28
Purchase of Weapons	30
Research and Development	13
Construction and Other	3

Another way of looking at the defense budget is by major mission. Items that cannot easily be attributed to particular missions, like research and training, account for much of the budget. Of the remainder, 16% is for "strategic" forces to deter and, if necessary, fight all-out nuclear war, while 84% is for what are called "general purpose" forces maintained for such duties as defending against a ground attack in Europe, invading Grenada, and maintaining a military presence throughout the world.

Strategic Forces. The mission of our strategic forces is to deter a nuclear attack on the United States and ensure that we retain the capacity to launch a devastating counter-attack against the aggressor. To achieve this capability, we rely upon land-based missiles, submarine-based missiles, and bombers.

The U.S. bomber fleet is several decades old, but still serviceable. However, technological advances in defenses against bomber attack suggest that much of the bomber fleet would no longer be able to reach heavily defended targets in the Soviet Union. Current and planned improvements in our airborne attack capacity include new bombers—the B-1B and an advanced technology (Stealth) bomber—and cruise missiles that would be launched by bombers operating outside Soviet air space. Current budget projections accommodate continued procurement of cruise missiles and B-1Bs, continuing development of the Stealth, and increased research and development on missile defense, including what has come to be known as the "Star Wars" program.

The level of spending needed for land-based strategic missiles is highly dependent upon whether our country wants a so-called "second-strike capability"—that is, the ability to absorb an initial attack and then retaliate effectively. Many consider this capacity to be essential. But today, the accuracy and number of Russian warheads are believed to be sufficient to destroy much of our land-based missile force, even if it were housed in silos like the ones used for the MX missile.

Thus, to absorb a first strike while retaining an assured counter-attack capability, the United States also needs submarine and air-based missiles. Since an enemy would have more difficulty locating these missiles, he could not guarantee that all U.S. retaliatory capability had been destroyed in the first attack. Therefore, he would be deterred from attacking because he could not be sure that the U.S. would be unable to launch a counterattack. However, many defense analysts worry that technological discoveries may eventually allow a potential adversary to detect, shadow, and destroy a greater percentage of U.S. missile-carrying submarines and aircraft.

To have assured second strike capability, it is generally agreed that land-based missiles must be mobile. Many different plans have been considered, such as putting missiles on rail cars or in a large system of silos, only a small percentage of which would be occupied at any one time. The President's current plan is to buy new (MX) missiles to replace existing (Minuteman) missiles and to deploy the MX in existing silos while seeking strategic arms limitation agreements with the Soviets. While this is going on, the U.S. would also begin development and deployment of a small, mobile missile dubbed the "midgetman." At the same time, the U.S. would also be upgrading its submarine-based missile capabilities, including procurement of a new Trident submarine every year and replacing its Trident missiles with new ones.

General Purpose Forces. The size and cost of other American forces is critically dependent upon two factors: (1) the magnitude and duration of the most difficult mission planned for those forces and (2) the minimum excess capacity needed during the most difficult mission to handle other threatening situations.

In military planning over the past several decades, the most demanding mission has been joining our NATO allies in the defense of Europe against a ground attack from Warsaw Pact nations in a military action lasting a considerable period of time. Preparation for this contingency requires stationing Army and Air Force units in Europe and pre-positioning supplies and equipment for additional units that would be airlifted from the United States. For such a conflict, it is assumed that a much larger naval force would be required to protect the sea lanes. It is further assumed that the United States would want to leave troops and ships deployed in the Pacific. It is generally agreed that any U.S. force with this capability would be able to handle other needs that might arise.

Given this mission, the assumption that Warsaw Pact countries will fight as a unit, and the current military posture of our European allies, the required general purpose force budget is expensive. Even with all of the defense spending currently planned, it is not clear that NATO could stop the Warsaw Pact from a successful ground attack in Europe without employing nuclear weapons. (It is clear that considerably more spending than is now planned would be required to tackle the more ambitious mission of being able to fight a successful conventional war with the Soviets in the Middle East.)

The budget projections provide for expenditures consistent with the European mission—pre-positioned supplies in Europe for additional divisions, more air transport capacity, more sea transport capacity, purchase of 150 or more F-16s each year for the rest of the decade, over 700 new M-1 tanks a year, even more Bradley fighting vehicles (the successor to armored personnel carriers), new Navy fighters, continued ship procurement looking toward a 600–ship navy, plus research and development on new tactical weapons systems. Given the importance of deterring—or if necessary repelling—an attack against the NATO allies in Europe, the President and Congress have felt a sense of urgency about this pace of procurement. While most of our conventional weapons are considered the equal of Warsaw Pact weapons, not all of our troops have these weapons. Furthermore, fighting a conventional war in Europe assumes the use of National Guard units, many of which have weapons quite obsolete by our standards and, more important, by the Soviets'.

Approaches to Defense Spending. Making a major reduction in the Defense Department budget by changing missions would require a decision that we would no longer strive for the capacity necessary to repel a Warsaw Pact ground attack in Europe by conventional means. This reduction could rest on one of two new policies: (1) that the U.S. would meet conventional aggression in Europe primarily with nuclear weapons or

(2) that the U.S. would make an affordable commitment to European defense, but the decision of whether total NATO capacity was adequate or not would be left to those with the largest stake in the outcome—European governments.

Members of Congress and mainstream critics of defense spending have been very reluctant to question the key strategic and conventional missions driving the defense budget. Instead, they have concentrated on concepts of affordable defense spending and appropriate rates of growth in inflation-adjusted defense spending.

One approach to defense spending is historical. The implicit premise behind this approach is that comparing past and present patterns is an appropriate way to judge current policy.

In constant 1982 dollar (inflation-adjusted) terms, the defense budget declined from the Vietnam War era to 1977, as Table 4.5 indicates. However, in the wake of congressional approval of President Reagan's defense spending proposals, the defense budget grew by 40% in real terms between FY 1981 and FY 1986. Most of the increased spending has been for research, development and procuring new weapons sys-

TABLE 4.5
REAL DEFENSE SPENDING

	Constant 1982 Dollars	Percent of GNP		Constant 1982 Dollars	Percent of GNP
1967	235.1	9.0	1980	164.0	5.0
1968	254.8	9.6	1981	171.4	5.3
1969	243.4	8.9	1982	185.3	5.9
1970	225.6	8.3	1983	201.3	6.3
1971	202.7	7.5	1984	211.5	6.2
1972	190.9	6.9	1985	228.7	6.4
1973	175.1	6.0	1986	242.1	6.6
1974	163.3	5.6	1987	242.6	6.4
1975	159.8	5.7	1988	246.9	6.3
1976	153.6	5.3	1989	250.2	6.2
1977	154.3	5.0	1990	256.0	6.1
1978	155.0	4.8	1991	263.6	6.0
1979	159.1	4.8			

tems. According to the Office of Management and Budget, real defense spending is expected to slow to a 3% rate of growth between 1988 and 1991. (By comparison, the Congressional Budget Office estimates that if real defense spending is held constant between now and 1991, outlays in 1991 will be $38 billion below the Administration's projections.)

The history of defense spending can also be calculated by examining the historical trend of defense outlays measured as a percentage of GNP. During the Vietnam War, outlays for defense rose to 9.6% of GNP, then fell gradually to 4.8% of GNP in 1979. They are currently about 6.5%, and scheduled to decline to 6.0% of GNP under the Administration's 3% real growth assumptions. Outlays will be an even lower percentage of GNP if real defense spending grows more slowly than 3% per year.

There is a general belief that all government agencies in general and the Defense Department in particular could be run more efficiently, getting more performance out of any given spending level. However, it is difficult to translate this belief into specific proposals. When this is done, as it was by the Grace Commission, the resulting savings estimates are widely criticized as unrealistic.

The operations and maintenance and military personnel components of the defense budget are basically a function of the size of the active forces. However, a major reduction of active forces in any of the three services would be inconsistent with a European conventional war mission. Reductions in the investment portion of the budget (construction, research and development, and procurement) are, in a sense, easier to make because the stated rationale can simply be the postponement of capabilities, not their total elimination. Besides delaying the availability of weapons, however, this stretch-out strategy often increases their unit price by forcing inefficient production levels. Hence, a stretch-out can be very expensive in the long run, even though it saves some outlays immediately.

Assuming that partly finished projects are not canceled, cuts in procurement spending have little effect on outlays in the year for which the budget is being cut. Major weapons, particularly ships and aircraft, have long lead times, so most of the actual procurement spending in any year is the result of spending authorizations in prior years. Decisions to cut FY 1988 budget authority for procurement would be felt primarily in FY 1989 and beyond.

Foreign Aid

In recent years, the U.S. has been spending about $15 billion for foreign aid. About $10 billion is closely tied to the defense budget. The security assistance portion of the foreign aid budget finances military and economic aid to a variety of friends and allies such as South Korea. This portion of the foreign aid budget could be reduced, but only if we were willing to accept a lower level of military capability in the countries we are supporting with military assistance. This in turn would mean relying more heavily on U.S. forces if these countries were attacked.

The remaining $5 billion in the foreign aid budget is for economic assistance. It is not directly tied to defense needs of the recipient. This item includes U.S. contributions to multi-lateral development institutions such as the World Bank that make loans to less-developed countries, as well as direct economic aid. All or part of this assistance could be ended, at the expense both of improved living standards in less developed countries (which enhance their ability to purchase our exports) and of our ability to influence the decisions of their leaders.

The Safety Net

Most Americans believe that the government should pay for a safety net that guarantees a minimum level of social services to the truly needy. Before someone can receive this assistance, they are required to prove that they are poor. Such programs, therefore, are known as "means-tested." In 1986, the federal government spent approximately $70 billion on these safety net programs. If there is no change in current policy, spending for these programs is projected to rise to $96 billion by FY 1991. The major federal means-tested programs with their projected FY 1991 spending levels are:

Medicaid ($39.4 billion, plus substantial state and local contributions): States administer health care assistance for all welfare recipients plus other low income individuals. This program reimburses states for a portion of the cost they incur in providing these medical services to the poor.

Food Stamps ($13.9 billion): The poor are given food stamps which they can use to purchase food from grocery stores.

Supplemental Security Income ($13.5 billion): Persons over 65, the aged, blind, and disabled are given cash assistance. The precise payment such persons receive depends on their income.

Assistance Payments ($11.5 billion plus substantial state and local contributions): This is what most people think of as welfare. The major program in this category, Aid to Families with Dependent Children, provides monthly payments to low-income single parents and, in some states, to couples when both parents are unemployed.

Child Nutrition ($5.3 billion): There is a range of programs designed to provide food to needy children, of which the school lunch program is the largest.

Veterans' Pensions ($3.7 billion): Certain needy veterans are entitled to pensions.

Other Means-Tested Programs ($9.0 billion): A variety of smaller programs are means-tested. Guaranteed college student loans are the largest program in this category.

Those who favor cuts in these programs argue that while their motive and stated goals are worthy, many of them simply do not work as well as intended. They make people dependent on hand-outs, leave them trapped in a vicious cycle of poverty, and create dependency rather than independence. Thus, despite the billions of dollars spent on these programs, they do not do the poor any good and therefore, they should be cut back.

Opponents of cutting these programs note that they have absorbed most of the cuts during the past six years. It is not fair for them to absorb still more reductions. In addition, they point out that these programs are under attack, not because they represent waste and fraud, but because they help the least politically powerful segments of society—the poor, the disadvantaged, and young people. We should not be balancing the budget at their expense, especially if it means denying them better access to decent housing, medical care, or an education.

Other Programs

The other major federal government programs, along with CBO's baseline FY 1991 projected spending levels, are:

TABLE 4.6
FY 1991 OUTLAY PROJECTIONS

Function	Cost ($ Billions)
General Science, Space and Technology	12
Energy	5
Natural Resources and Environment	17
Agriculture	23
Commerce and Housing Credit	5
Transportation	31
Community and Regional Development	7
Education, Training, Employment, and Social Services	38
Veterans' Benefits and Services	29
Administration of Justice	10
General Government	8
General Purpose Fiscal Assistance	2

Some of the largest costs on this list are for paying pensions to retired employees—veterans, civil servants, and special groups like railroad workers. Some people believe that these retirement benefits are too generous and should be scaled back. However, current retirees are being paid only what they were promised when they took the job in the first place. Therefore, unless we are going to renege on these promises, benefit reductions should be confined primarily to newly hired workers. Unfortunately, while this might save the government considerable money in the future, it will have little effect on spending levels before 1991.

However, many current retirees do receive annual cost of living increases. About $5.5 billion would be saved in FY 1991 if COLAs covered only two-thirds of annual inflation. In addition, some of the more expensive and rapidly growing costs for veterans are unrelated to any disability they might have acquired while serving in the armed forces. Confining veterans benefits (particularly free health care) to those whose health problems are service-connected would save about $1.7 billion.

Another major federal government spending program is targeted at farmers. Since the Great Depression, the U.S. government has agreed that farmers should be protected, at least in part, against income declines caused by falling prices for the crops they grow. Through a variety of techniques, the government has tried to guarantee farmers a certain price for their crops or a certain income irrespective of the price they receive for their crops. At times, the government has paid farmers not to grow as much of a particular crop, on the theory that a smaller supply will raise the price for the portion that is produced and sold.

The cost of these agricultural subsidies has skyrocketed in recent years. In 1981, the federal government spent approximately $4 billion on agricultural price support programs. Today, the cost of those same programs is more than $20 billion. Cutting back these farm subsidies could save anywhere from $6.5 billion to $18.6 billion, depending on the precise array of policy reforms that are adopted.

Supporters of these policy reforms note that while their cost has skyrocketed, the programs have done little to prevent bankruptcies and economic dislocation in rural America. Thus, it is clear that, despite their expense, they are not promoting the long-term prosperity of the agricultural sector. Moreover, because the size of the subsidy is pegged to the volume of production, a few very large farmers receive the bulk of the payments.

Opponents of cutting these programs argue that they help to

preserve our domestic food production capacity, which is essential to our national security. They also point out that farmers are going out of business in record numbers, and hundreds of farm banks are on the verge of failure. With such severe problems down on the farm, this is the worst possible time to contemplate eliminating government assistance.

The remaining category covers such operating expenses of the federal government as collecting taxes, running the Congress, maintaining national parks, operating the Coast Guard, etc. Outlays for these types of activities will be about $50 billion in 1991. Budget projections assume that spending for them, primarily for federal wages and benefits, will grow to match inflation. However, cutting the size of the federal work force and scaling back a portion of the scheduled pay increases could save close to $3.6 billion by 1991.

Asset Sales

In recent budgets, President Reagan has added asset sales to the Administration's deficit reduction package. Under the terms of this proposal, the federal government would finance a portion of its spending, not via taxes or borrowing, but by selling federal government assets to private investors. The proceeds could then be used to pay for government programs, just as tax proceeds or bond sales do now.

In 1986, Congress, agreed to sell the government-owned freight railroad, Conrail. It is expected that proceeds from that sale will add $2.2 billion to the federal government's coffers. Congress also agreed to sell a number of loan assets with an estimated face value of $7.2 billion. If completed, sales of these assets would generate an estimated $4.8 billion for the federal treasury.

Under this plan, the federal government will sell to private investors a portion of the loans made by various federal agencies, including the Small Business Administration and the Export-Import Bank. Since these loans tend to be riskier than typical loans made by private sector lenders and because their interest rate is generally lower than the rate that private sector

borrowers would charge, the federal government cannot obtain
$100 for each $100 loan. Instead, it will receive somewhat less,
perhaps only $60 or $70. Nevertheless, proponents of loan
sales point out that they are a way of raising government
receipts without raising taxes. And these extra receipts, they
point out, reduce the deficit on the same dollar for dollar basis
as a tax increase or spending reduction.

Opponents are not so sure. They point out that during the
life of the loan, the federal government would be receiving
interest and principal repayments from the borrowers. These
repayment streams count as government revenues during each
year they are received. By selling these loans today, the
government will be giving up the right to receive these future
interest and principal payments. Hence, the government will
be reducing the deficit today, but at the cost of increasing the
deficit tomorrow. Passing the buck to future generations is
precisely the sort of policy that generated the current deficits.
Those same buck-passing policies should not now be seen as a
way out of the morass.

In addition, critics of asset sales note that they do not reduce
the government's claim over private sector resources. Instead
of paying taxes or buying U.S. government bonds, the private
sector will be spending its money on government assets.
Money that was originally in the private sector still ends up in
the federal treasury. For this reason, the Congressional Budget
Office noted recently that asset sales, "squeeze credit markets
in almost the same fashion as borrowing by the federal government. The amount paid for the asset is no more available for
private investment than is a like amount loaned to the Treasury."

Finally, critics note that loan asset sales do not alter the
long term trajectory, or imbalance, between revenues and
expenditures. They are a one-shot bonus. They do nothing to
alter the fact that spending remains above revenues. All they
do is allow Congress and the President to pretend that they are
reaching the Gramm-Rudman targets when in fact they are
doing so only by fancy, and somewhat misleading, bookkeep-
ing techniques.

Summary

While the federal budget is large and complex, its magnitude is largely controlled by a few decisions.

Defense costs can be reduced by identifying objectives that could be altered to save money. Failing this, and lacking an easy way to identify and cut "waste," Congress affects the defense budget primarily through decisions on how fast to buy new weapons.

Social Security can be excluded from consideration on principle, as some advocate. But if some reductions are deemed necessary, the primary short-term choice is whether to provide recipients with full protection from inflation and whether benefits should continue to enjoy substantial tax advantages. For Medicare and Social Security, there is also the question of whether affluent people should get benefits and to what extent these benefits should be taxed.

The remaining issues must either be dealt with individually, or some general logic—like the idea of a general means test or a "freeze" on spending growth—must be applied to all of them.

CHAPTER 5

Towards More Responsible Budget Policies

Introduction: Brief History of Current Budget Policies

As noted earlier, the Constitution provides that money cannot be spent by federal officials except under an "appropriation" of funds made by Congress. Congress makes funds available by passing appropriations bills, the legislation by which the spending part of the budget is enacted. For most of our history, Congress carried out these responsibilities by dealing directly with the heads of federal agencies and military commanders. Each agency chief submitted his budget directly to Congress, frequently by-passing the President altogether.

As the government became larger, however, this decentralized procedure was considered to be too unwieldy. Accordingly, in the 1920s, Congress mandated that the agencies submit their budgets directly to the President. The President was then supposed to sift through the various requests and establish the Administration's spending priorities for that year, deciding what items should receive full funding and which ones should be put on a back burner or rejected outright. The complete set of Presidential decisions and priorities was then transmitted to Congress as "the budget." The theory behind this approach was that the President was in the best position to compare the needs of one agency with those of all the others and to arrive at an overall spending plan based on the money likely to be available from existing revenue sources plus any new revenues he might care to recommend.

While this law required the President to consider the budget in its totality and to balance competing spending and revenue claims, it did not impose a parallel responsibility on Congress. As Congress made its decisions either to approve, reject, or amend the President's proposals, it considered the budget in piecemeal fashion. Each year, it would vote on 13 separate appropriations bills. But Congress was under no obligation to consider how the cumulative weight of those 13 separate spending decisions would affect total federal spending—or the deficit. The only thing Congress knew for sure was how much money it was voting at that particular moment for that particular agency.

Congress also had no way of knowing whether projected revenues would be adequate to finance those appropriations. Nobody in Congress was keeping score of how much money was being appropriated and therefore, how much money would be needed to pay for that spending. Complicating matters was the fact that decisions about raising revenues were made by the House Ways and Means Committee and the Senate Finance Committee, not the appropriations committees. Consequently, spending and revenue decisions were made independently and without any formal mechanism for coordinating the two halves of the budget.

Finally, the appropriations committees did not have jurisdiction over every federal spending program. Entitlement programs were handled by Ways and Means and Finance. Still other committees had indirect jurisdiction over spending through their power to change the authorizing legislation (e.g., eligibility requirements for certain benefits, etc.). And when Congress wanted to bypass the appropriations committees altogether, it would enact what was known as "backdoor spending."

Under this procedure, Congress would authorize an agency to issue loan guarantees which obligated the federal government to repay the loan if the private sector borrower defaulted or went bankrupt. This allowed individuals who were poor credit risks to borrow money directly from private lenders. From Congress' point of view, loan guarantees had one major advantage over direct appropriations: Since a bankruptcy or default would not ordinarily occur for several years, Congress could funnel money immediately into the coffers of favored projects, secure in the belief that the bill for those loan guarantees would not come due for several years at the earliest. At that point Congress and the President would have no choice except to approve an appropriation to honor the loan guarantee.

Congressional Budget Procedures: Post-1974

Because there was no centralized budget process, and because all these various pieces of legislation were handled by different committees, Members could easily rail against deficits and also vote for higher spending. They could vote for tax cuts and expenditure increases without ever voting directly on the deficit that would inevitably result. Members of Congress, in other words, could cast votes that had the effect of creating deficits without ever voting explicitly for a deficit.

Concern over this problem led Congress in 1974 to establish the budget procedure described earlier in Chapter 2. Many people believe that the new procedures have helped Congress become aware of the tradeoffs between spending more for one program and the need either to raise taxes or vote explicitly for the resulting deficit. With the current budget process and the need to pass a budget resolution, Congress at least knows the implications of what it is doing before it does it. Somebody in Congress—the Congressional Budget Office (CBO)—has the task of keeping score and tallying the cost of the decisions.

In theory, this additional information should help individual Members of Congress make more rational and informed budget decisions. The theory may be correct, but the evidence shows that the current budget process has neither prevented unbalanced budgets nor reduced the size of the deficits, as Table 5.1 indicates. The average size of budget deficits has increased in each succeeding five year period since the end of World

TABLE 5.1

DEFICITS OVER TIME

	Years Without Deficits	Average Deficit	Smallest Deficit	Largest Deficit
PHASE I BUDGET PROCEDURE				
1946–1950	3	−0.52	+11.8 (SURPLUS)	−15.9
1951–1955	1	−1.22	+6.1 (SURPLUS)	−6.5
1956–1960	3	−1.60	+3.9 (SURPLUS)	−12.8
1961–1965	0	−4.50	−1.4	−7.1
1966–1970	1	−7.40	+3.2 (SURPLUS)	−25.1
1971–1975	0	−24.10	−6.1	−53.2
PHASE II BUDGET PROCEDURE				
1976–1980	0	−60.06	−40.1	−73.8
1981–1985	0	−162.62	−78.9	−212.2

War II. The largest increase—nearly $100 billion—occurred between 1981 and 1986.

Congressional Budget Procedure: Gramm-Rudman-Hollings

According to many observers, the Gramm-Rudman-Hollings bill should be seen as a last ditch attempt to instill discipline into the budget process. Even with the 1974 budget reforms, there was still too much fragmentation of authority and lack of accountability. There was no system to force Congress to enact the specific legislation needed to make the budget resolution a reality. The budget resolution could not compel the tax writing committees to approve tax increases, and even if the committees complied, individual Members of Congress were under no legal obligation to vote for the specific tax bill reported by the Committee. Everyone could be in favor of a tax increase in general and oppose the specific measure under consideration.

Similar problems existed on the spending side of the ledger.

As a general rule, a Congressman could favor spending reductions and still disapprove of the precise spending cuts under debate. Thus, even the new budget procedures gave Members a way to have their cake and eat it too. They could vote for small deficits and spending cuts during the debate on the budget resolution and then vote for specific legislation that generated spending increases and large deficits.

Gramm-Rudman-Hollings does not tackle these problems directly. Instead it says that irrespective of the decision making process Congress used or the votes that were taken on specific bills, the deficit must be eliminated by 1993. To guarantee this result, as we have seen, Gramm-Rudman-Hollings establishes a sequestration process that both gives Congress and the President incentives to reach agreement on annual deficit reductions and ensures automatic budget cuts in the event they cannot agree.

The Line Item Veto

Some argue that the entire sequestration process is irrational. Although they believe that spending should be cut, they do not think that it makes sense to cut every program by the same percentage. Not every program is of equal importance. Some are more crucial than others. With this in mind, they suggest that if Congress cannot set its own priorities, the President should be given additional powers so that he can set them instead. One of the most frequently mentioned powers is the line item veto, which 43 governors have, but which the President does not.

At present, the President only has the power to sign or veto entire bills. If he uses his veto, the bill can become law anyway, but only if Congress overrides the veto by mustering a two-thirds majority in both houses. The veto is a powerful instrument for exercising presidential power. However, it is not a particularly effective tool for dealing with appropriations bills, since these are typically passed shortly before the affected agencies are set to run out of money.

This deadline puts strong pressures on the President to reach an accommodation with the Congress so that the agencies do not have to shut down. To make matters worse, in recent years, the Congress has combined several appropriations bills into one large omnibus "continuing resolution." This forces the President to choose between wielding the veto and shutting down several agencies or accepting spending programs that are not precisely to his liking.

With a line item veto, the President would not be faced with this choice since he would not have to accept or veto an entire appropriations bill. Instead, he would be able to veto only those items he dislikes and sign the remaining provisions. As with any veto, a two-thirds vote of Congress could override the line item veto and restore the original funding levels.

Because a line item veto would allow the President to reduce spending but never increase it, many people who seek lower federal spending support the item veto. Opponents fear that it would give the President too much power. Instead, they think it is better for the President to negotiate with Congressional leaders over the spending cuts he wants.

The Balanced Budget Amendment

Some people believe that the only solution for escalating deficits is an amendment to the Constitution requiring the President and Congress to balance the budget every year. Forty-nine of the 50 states and most local governments have this sort of provision in their constitutions. The provision most commonly advocated for inclusion in the U.S. Constitution would require the budget to be balanced every year, except during national emergencies declared by a two-thirds vote of Congress.

Opponents of the balanced budget amendment include some groups that support higher federal spending for such objectives as education and federal employee pay and pensions. But other opponents have more general objections. Some believe that deficits are necessary to help the economy avoid recessions and to alleviate recessions once they begin. Still others believe that while a constant stream of large deficits may be bad for the economy, this does not mean that a constant stream of balanced budgets is the appropriate alternative. As the discussion in Chapter 2 pointed out, there is wide disagreement over both the definition of an appropriate deficit and the speed with which the government should be required to achieve those deficit levels.

A balanced budget amendment would outlaw all deficits, even if the conventional wisdom agreed that some moderate level of deficits is desirable. And it would not necessarily set a reasonable glide path for reaching that appropriate level. Therefore, opponents believe it could do more harm than good. Still others who are supporters of balanced budgets believe that the Constitution should be a place where broad fundamental precepts of government are spelled out, not where less consequential housekeeping details are discussed.

Changing the Process in Congress

The Congressional budget process clearly has not worked as well as its sponsors intended. Not surprisingly, a number of people have suggested that Congress needs to consider changing some of the housekeeping techniques it uses to manage the federal budget.

Some people believe that trying to pass a budget every year simply overwhelms the creaky Congressional decision making process. No sooner does Congress finish with this year's budget than it has to start work on next year's budget. The pressures of trying to pass a budget resolution, authorization legislation, 13 appropriations bills, and revenue measures on a year-in, year-out basis does not leave enough time to determine whether programs are working as intended or to investigate whether there are more cost-effective ways of delivering government services. Thus, some people suggest that Congress should operate on a two year budget cycle. The first year of every Congress would be devoted to passing a budget for the next two years. The second year could then be devoted to other matters.

Other suggestions for housekeeping improvements focus on

ways to eliminate the division of labor between authorizing committees and the appropriations committees. Critics of the current procedures note that it fragments decision making and makes it more difficult to carry out the intent of the budget resolution. Each additional step creates new opportunities for opponents to block enactment of a particular spending cut. If they lose a vote during consideration of the budget resolution, they can try again during the vote on the authorization bill. And if they lose during the authorizing process, they can make one last-ditch attempt at keeping the program alive during the appropriations committee's deliberations.

For this reason, Congressional critics argue that as long as responsibility for enacting a budget is split among so many committees, actually approving specific budget cuts will be more difficult than it ought to be. To reduce these obstacles, some have suggested combining the authorization and appropriations committees. Under this proposal, the people setting up the program and establishing its eligibility requirements would also be in charge of appropriating funds for its operation. The hope is that by streamlining the budget process, there would be fewer opportunities to sabotage budget cuts and greater coordination between the budget resolution's provisions and the eventual spending decisions made by Congress.

Opponents of both measures do not necessarily object to the procedural changes *per se*. They simply note that more streamlined decision making will not necessarily result in lower deficits and more responsible budgets. Therefore, they argue, while various housekeeping changes may be desirable, these procedural issues should not divert attention from efforts to achieve a more far-reaching reform.

The Power of Public Opinion

While all of these changes have certain advantages, the most important single factor in our democratic country is what the American people think. More precisely, the important thing is what representatives of the people in Congress think the people think.

One of the problems Congress has is that it rarely hears from the average person. Instead, the people who write to Members usually have a particular interest. This means when it is examining spending, Congress tends to hear from people who want to spend money. When it considers spending for education it hears from parents, teachers, and professional advocates of education. When it considers spending for health care, it hears from doctors and other health care professionals. When it considers taxes, Congress hears from taxpayers who care about different provisions of the tax law but have in common their desire to avoid tax increases affecting them and to reduce their taxes if they can. Thus, if Congress lets spending outrun revenue and creates a big deficit, it is doing what the people seem to be telling it to do.

It is not surprising that few people have communicated forcefully with their representatives about the overall deficits. Our nation has little experience with peacetime deficits at current high levels. We have no experience with large deficits significantly financed by capital from other nations. Furthermore, most people do not understand the complex procedures used to generate the federal budget.

Now that the 1988 presidential elections are on the horizon, the federal budget deficit has moved to the forefront of public policy debate. It is clear that economic recovery alone will not soon lead to a balanced budget and that the very survival of the recovery may be imperiled by the deficit. Most polls indicate that the American people are deeply concerned about the deficit. These same polls suggest that the people are uncertain about the origins of the deficit and deeply divided about ways to remedy it. Whether the elections will produce new policies from elected public officials depends almost entirely on the kinds of messages they receive from the ultimate source of power in our political system—citizens who work, pay taxes, receive public services, and vote.

51 58